YANO

YANO

From the Prune Ranch to Skyscrapers

A Sicilian-American Shares Lessons in Success

John "Mariano" Michael Rubino

iUniverse, Inc.
New York Lincoln Shanghai

YANO
From the Prune Ranch to Skyscrapers

Copyright © 2007 by John Rubino

iUniverse books may be ordered through booksellers or by contacting:

iUniverse
2021 Pine Lake Road, Suite 100
Lincoln, NE 68512
www.iuniverse.com
1-800-Authors (1-800-288-4677)

Edited by Heather Hutson Moro

Paintings by John Rubino

Painting photography by Sandro Moro

ISBN: 978-0-595-43148-9 (pbk)
ISBN: 978-0-595-68210-2 (cloth)
ISBN: 978-0-595-87492-7 (ebk)

Printed in the United States of America

I dedicate this book to my parents:
Giuseppina and Giuseppe Rubino
They instilled in me the love of and faith in God!

TABLE OF CONTENTS

FOREWORD

My intentions were simple the day I met John Rubino. As a freelance editor fresh off of maternity leave—and with a four-month-old baby needing my attention—I arrived at John's house intending to review his book draft and related materials, give him my feedback, advise him on what his next move should be, and be on my way.

Here's what happened instead. John gave me a tour of his meticulously collected memorabilia, all laid out in thirty-seven binders on his dining room table. As a busy new mom, the thirty-seven binders should have sent me running for the door (they very nearly did). But instead, I realized I was beginning to feel the effects of this man's overwhelming enthusiasm and positive outlook—and I began to wonder whether this attitude, plus his general openness to experience and opportunity, weren't magic qualities I needed to understand better.

I began to see that this man had led a successful, happy, and interesting life, and that he had done so not just through hard work and determination (though there's no shortage of these), but also by having faith and optimism, being a willing and generous soul, and saying yes to opportunities that were presented to him.

I couldn't help thinking of the Richard Scarry children's story of Pig Will and Pig Won't, in *Richard Scarry's Please and Thank You Book*. Pig Will always says "I will!" when asked to do something, and Pig Won't always says (you guessed it) "I won't." In the story, Pig Will agrees to help his father work on his boat, while Pig Won't, of course, refuses. The outcome: Pig Will has a fabulous time—meeting all sorts of characters down at the shipyard, learning how to do things like pound nails and varnish water skis, and getting ice cream as a treat. In the mean time, Pig Won't sits at home, moping and bored.

I realized that I, like Pig Won't, have a tendency to say no. I turn down opportunities when I'm not certain where they may lead. I tend to think negatively about them: to fear the worst—that I will fail, that I will agree to do something but then let someone down. That fear saves me from making mistakes, sure. But it also prevents me—and perhaps you?—from taking paths in life that could lead us toward our own definition of success and happiness.

I decided that day *not* to say no—at least not to the opportunity to work with John Rubino on his memoir, and to learn what I could from his life. And it was the right choice: I soon recognized a number of valuable lessons inherent in his stories, and encouraged John to arrange his memoir in a way that highlights them. We also decided to include a "practice" question or prompt at the end of each chapter, encouraging readers to consider how each lesson might apply to them. Throughout all this, I was discovering the value of a positive outlook, of maintaining friendships and business connections, and of saying yes and being ready to offer assistance.

As you read this book, may you also find lessons you can apply to your own life. (Do I hear an "I will"?)

Heather Hutson Moro, Editor
December 2006

ACKNOWLEDGMENTS

Thanks and Praise

This is my opportunity to express gratitude to all those who have influenced and made a contribution to my life. I feel blessed to have so many people to thank! I have attempted to give thanks and recognition to different individuals within the various chapters of this book and within these acknowledgments. However, there are so many more who have played an important role in my life ... there is no way I can mention everyone by name. I would like to extend my apologies to anyone who may have been left out, as well as my thanks to all who have touched my life.

I begin these acknowledgments as I begin each day: thanking God for giving me this wonderful gift of life! I am also grateful for the following key people who have influenced my journey.

Heather Hutson Moro, freelance editor and writer who showed great insight and passion for this book. Her devotion and expertise throughout the entire process made me refer to her as "My Angel." She is very gifted and talented. Thank you, Heather, and thanks to Sandy Silva, your aunt, who recommended you to me!

Henry J. Kaiser, my inspiration to join the Kaiser organization. I applaud Cornell Maier, who played an instrumental role in organizing the Henry J. Kaiser: THINK BIG exhibit at the Oakland Museum.

John Renard, President of Cushman & Wakefield, who was my mentor and my reason to join the Cushman & Wakefield organization.

My wonderful family:

o My sister, Marianna, and nephew and godchild Ronald Crosetti. When I began to write for my book about my brush with death during the 1989 Loma Prieta Earthquake, Ronald amazingly remembered all the facts and times of the events!

o My brother, Joe, and his wife, Pat, who recently celebrated fifty years of marriage—a true love story!

o Their children:

▪ My niece and godchild Gina and her daughter, Olivia.

- My niece Josette and her husband, Jeff Kruljac, and sons Dominic and Justin.
- My nephew Bob and his wife, Vickie.
o Theresa Vera, enthusiastic and loyal family friend.

I am so pleased to be invited to all the family birthday parties, holidays, and special events. I am never alone!

The Greco and Rubino families in Trabia, Sicily, who I have been fortunate to visit twice in my life. Fantastic memories!

Frank Terranova and his wife, Valerie. Frank is my Fort Ord buddy, and he and his wife are lifetime friends who encouraged me to publish my life story.

Their daughter, Nancy Terranova, my loving godchild.

Frank B. Blum, Jr., lawyer and friend, who also wanted me to persist in my writing. He was impressed with my many photos and experiences, and his wife, Nikki, has been especially helpful.

Ralph and Connie Weber, lifetime friends whose kindness and generosity I will never forget.

René and Gigi Bopp and Pierre-Bernard Buser and their families in Switzerland—special lifetime friends.

Anthony J. Errico, D.P.M., F.A.C.F.A.S., Certified American Board of Podiatric Surgery, and June Lovotti, his lovely and caring assistant. They have been members of my "fan club," cheering me on with my writing!

Manny, my barber for over thirty years, who encourages me with my book project.

Joe's of Westlake. This is a great restaurant, in business for over fifty years. Thanks to a wonderful, caring staff: Barry, John, Norma, Gloria, Jeff, Giovanni, George, Gus, Margaret, and others, and a great cook, Tony! My mother loved Joe's, and they loved my mother!

Other key people and organizations I am grateful to include:

Miss Mildred C. Cavanagh, Paul Revere Grammar School teacher, who motivated me to attend college.

The Kiwanis Club of San Francisco, which awarded me a $2,000 college scholarship. Eugene Lorton, Chairman of the Scholarship Committee, was very helpful and generous with his advice regarding my career goals.

Bob and Rita Gaddini and Jean Weingand are special friends dating back to Commerce High School days. We have gotten together for delightful lunches in Novato (the Gaddini residence), and I have treated them at Joe's of Westlake when they have come to Daly City.

Roland Quintero, a close friend of mine at Commerce High School and at the University of California at Berkeley. He and his wife, Elizabeth, celebrated their fiftieth wedding anniversary, and Billy Quintero, my godchild, invited me to join him and his parents at this wonderful family event at a hotel in Palo Alto, California. Roland is a very talented professional photographer. He and Elizabeth make a great team. I value their friendship!

Robert G. Sproul, a very caring and effective president of the University of California at Berkeley. I treasure my meetings with him and his involvement with my campus activities.

Dean E. T. Grether (Business Administration) and Professor Kidner (Economics), who played significant roles in my Ph.D. studies in Economics and Business Administration at the University of California, Berkeley.

Peter Armanini, who I shared an adventure of a lifetime with during our Army service in 1954. I was in Peter's wedding upon our return home.

Dante Marcolina, another close and caring friend in the Army. Dante and his wife, Doris, invited me to their beautiful home in Marin County after we were discharged.

Colonel McGowan of the Inspector General in Salzburg, Austria, and the office staff (military and civilian) and other officers on the Inspector General team. Everyone was so supportive. Thank you, all!

Pablo (Paul) Perez, a great friend!

Henry Caruso, who used to have great parties at his home after Frank Terranova and I got out of the service. Pablo, Frank, and I enjoyed ourselves. Henry was a wonderful host!

Frank Scarr, mentor, who hired me as Chief Accountant of Kaiser Center.

Sylvia Vlahos, Secretary to Frank Scarr. We shared memorable Kaiser Center events.

Al Bava, Controller for Kaiser Center. Al was a great teacher of practical applications of accounting management.

Tim Preece, President of Kaiser Center, Inc. He encouraged me to develop my ideas and to grow professionally. Thank you, Tim!

Bonnie Guiton, Vice President of Kaiser Center, Inc., encouraged me to be my best and to be very active in community and public relations activities. She spearheaded my wonderful retirement party. Thank you, Bonnie!

JoAnne Kearns, my talented assistant who shared and contributed to many outstanding events and projects in Kaiser Center.

Colin Davies, a gifted writer and photographer for *Newsbreak*.

Kaiser executives A. B. Ordway, Gene Trefethen, Steve Girard, Bob Ver Steeg, Jim McCloud, Dick Spees, H. T. Warren, Carl Pagter, Bill Holzwarth, Peter S. Hass, Dr. Clifford H. Keene, and Jim Vohs.

Attorneys Marvin Starr, Harry Miller, and Ed Regalia (Miller, Starr & Regalia).

George Vukasian, civic leader.

Mayor Lionel Wilson of Oakland.

Those who wrote special letters upon my retirement from Kaiser Center: John Hills, Director, Oakland Unified School District; Kenneth A. Sorensen, Managing Partner, Peat Marwick (CPA firm); St. John's Church and Reverend C. Eugene Sill; Burton Weber, City of Oakland Office of Parks and Recreation; Ellen and Walter Newman; E. T. Grether, Professor Emeritus, University of California, Berkeley; Richard Sprague; Paul B. Henne; and Stephen A. Girard, Kaiser Steel president.

The many wonderful people who attended my Kaiser retirement party. I was just thrilled and overwhelmed with gratitude, especially since my mother was there.

Cushman & Wakefield key players: Arthur Mirante, John Renard, Joe Cook, Jerry Lewis, Rich Larsen, Jeff Smith, Mike Bernatz, Richard Carcione, Sean Maher, Jim McPhee, and Dan Harvey.

Lake Merritt Plaza key players: Shurl Curci, owner; Peter Adams, president; Bill Cutler, marketing; Susan Munday, marketing. Susan, Jeff Smith, and I worked very closely on the leasing. We had great chemistry and not only enjoyed our work but we were very successful—we were a great team!

2101 Webster Street key players: Charles Pankow, owner; Mike Townsend, marketing; Ken Levy, executive with Matthew Bender (the building's major tenant).

Gene Englund, Touche Ross Auditors.

Irene Sargent, an important "leading lady." We worked together to "light Oakland on Broadway" for the Christmas in Oakland event.

Rosy Chu, host of *Channel 2—On the Square*. Rosy interviewed me live for the Christmas in Oakland activities in 1981. She was a delight to be interviewed by on the day of the parade. *On the Square* was a very popular local TV show, and I want to again thank Rosy Chu and Channel 2 KTVU for being so generous with their coverage. Rosy later sent me a videocassette of the interview—so thoughtful and kind. It's my treasure!

Diane Lichtenstein, my terrific assistant for "Showcase Oakland" when I was General Chairman.

Additional business contacts who I am grateful to have known and worked with: Dave Van Noy, Kaiser Foundation; George and Hazel Valentine, BOMA of Oakland; Marc Intermaggio, BOMA of San Francisco; Ed Zwolenkiewicz, Blue Cross; Bill Logan, Kaiser Permanente; Ed Zelinsky, BOMA (Oakland property owner); Jerry Maxwell, Kaiser Center; Ed Bianco, Kaiser Center; Elena Orsini, artist; Gus Petris, community leader; Chuck Schwyn, Deloitte, Haskins & Sells; Kurt Svensson, Westinghouse Elevator; and David Tripaldi, Coldwell Banker.

Many more important friends, organizations, supporters, and employees: Fred LaCosse and Terry Lowry; Burton Weber; Faye Potter; Marita Inchauspe; Eric Hubert; Kay Velick and her mother; Phil Schichilone; Nancy Perakis; Ray Gallagher; Charlie Arolla and Bob Engle of the Gemini Club; Carl Finley; Chris Marshall; Paul McKowen; Tony Zidich (successful and long-standing Daly City treasurer); Peter Stanwyck, attorney; Ernie Reddick, attorney; Billy Martin; Narsai David; Trade Club; BOMA; Oakland Jaycees and the Miss California and Miss Oakland pageants; John Dolby; Gail Holland; April and Frank Cassano; Crispina and Ian McDonald; Charlie Parker; Joe Morgan; Franco Nicosia; Ted Mah; Auburn D. ("Don") Lee; Ken Venturi; Franco and Mariuccia Fazio; Rotary Club #3 (Oakland); Lake Merritt Breakfast Club; Dr. Richard L. Caplin; Dr. Frank J. Farrell; Dr. Lee K. Schwartz; Dr. Thomas M. Swift; and George A. Ambus, DDS.

Wayne Lippman, CPA, who has provided me with great tax and financial advice for many years.

Jane Bachmann and Andrew Nagle of Fidelity, my financial advisers—they have been very helpful to me. In 1997 Jane personally got me through the "maze of options" and successfully customized my investment program. Andrew calls me to advise me of current conditions—wonderful service!

Paul and Eva Comi—wonderful friends! We met during a tour of Sicily in 2000 and enjoy getting together when they visit San Francisco.

Rachel Lelchuk, waitress for fifty-five years at Louis' diner at Point Lobos. This diner overlooks Sutro Baths at the Pacific Ocean near the Cliff House in San Francisco. Rachel retired in 2003 at age eighty-two. She is a delight, and I would always wait for a table that she would provide for me overlooking the ocean—a terrific view! She has a wonderful interest in books and would share her latest find with me, vividly describing her reading adventures. Rachel memorized my breakfast selections so I didn't even have to order. She would start me off with coffee and it was a "bottomless" cup—she knew when to pour me a refill. I wish her happiness in her retirement—a wonderful person. It's her turn to be waited on!

Hogan's Restaurant. Frank Terranova and I go frequently on Fridays to this great place located in the Produce Market in South San Francisco. Being Sicilian with a love for fruits and vegetables, Frank and I feel right at home with the produce trucks making deliveries to places like "Franzella's" and "Carcione." Pictures of famous athletes adorn the walls. Our favorite waitress always brings us two dishes of their great clam chowder! Usually we have the filet of sole—very fresh. I spent some time in produce markets as a child, so this place brings back memories for me.

Norman Vincent Peale and his organization, which was instrumental in inspiring me to remain enthusiastic and focused in my life. Whenever I needed encouragement, I would read something by Norman Vincent Peale, even just a leaflet. Writings about faith, enthusiasm, and so on would reenergize me and keep me centered.

Sons of Italy Foundation: Honorable Robert Messa, President, and Vincent Sarno, Chairman. I have regularly donated to the Sons of Italy Foundation because I believe in their mission! I would like to include excerpts from their newsletters:

- "Your gift gave a new generation of Italian-American scholars the resources to study and perpetuate our proud past."

- "We at the Sons of Italy Foundation know that our scholarship programs instill the love of our culture in our children and grandchildren."

- "We know that our cultural outreach efforts keep alive the spirit of our people."

Finally, I also want to extend appreciation to some recent "visionaries" close to home:

David Lukes, Kimco Management—developers of the new Westlake Shopping Center (a modern village).

Boulevard Café, the new restaurant on John Daly Boulevard—leading the way toward exciting architecture for the twenty-first century in Westlake, Daly City!

Adding to My Enjoyment of Each Day

- Watching *Regis & Kelly* while drinking coffee from the *LIVE with Regis & Kelly* coffee cup given to me by my niece Josette Kruljac
- Watching the Bay Area's Channel 2 News (Ross McGowan, Mark, Tori, Frank, Sal, Steve, Tom); local channels 3, 4, 5, and 7; Dr. Phil, Larry King, Letterman, Leno, and Oprah; *60 Minutes,* Tim Russert, and Charlie Rose; Dr. Charles Stanley on Sunday mornings; public television programs, Lawrence Welk, and cooking shows; Donald Trump's *The Apprentice*
- Reading the *San Francisco Chronicle*
- Following local sports: the Oakland A's and the San Francisco Giants baseball teams, the San Francisco 49ers and the Oakland Raiders (John Madden, Al Davis, Al Lo Cosale) football teams, and the Golden State Warriors basketball team
- Reading, music, and movies

- Dining
- Shopping
- Travel
- Photography, Art
- Museums
- Gardening
- My wonderful neighbors
- My family and friends!
- And faith in God

Behind the Scenes: The Research Process

Lastly, a brief snapshot of the work that went into this book.

Boxes and *boxes* of material accumulated during my lifetime were examined and organized. I have over thirty-five volumes containing copies of pictures and materials, with an index on the cover of most. Each volume contains about 200 items—over 7,000 items in all! *Supporting* these are volumes containing the original pictures and documents. I prepared a comprehensive inventory of these in a binder describing each volume's content.

I wrote my story longhand on my kitchen table. My editor, Heather Moro, typed it up and put it on a computer disk (she could read my writing! Thank God!).

Our Goal: to make my life story *flow*!

INTRODUCTION

Visualize orchards in springtime: the beautiful blossoms on the prune, apricot, cherry, peach, and almond trees. Breathe in the heady fragrance. Imagine personally picking the fresh, ripe fruits from these trees later in the warm summer sun, and enjoying their juicy sweetness.

I was born to Sicilian immigrant parents during the Great Depression, on June 4, 1930, into this wonderful environment. Our ranch was an orchard of prune trees surrounded by other orchards belonging to my relatives. It was a magnificent setting—truly a gift from God!

Yano: From the Prune Ranch to Skyscrapers is my unique life story, starting with the prune ranch in San Jose, California, and leading to an exciting career in skyscrapers.

The name "Yano" is short for "Mariano," and it's what I was called while I was growing up on the prune ranch. (In fact, many years later, I began signing my oil paintings "Yano.") As a young child on the ranch, I remember not only the beautiful blossoms on the trees and that wonderful fresh air, but also the freedom to run through the high grass in the fields. It was so peaceful, and there was a sense of family community. I remember it well!

My life up to now has been quite a journey, and I would like to share my experiences with you. I have been encouraged to write about my life's journey by family and friends. Even in my travels throughout the world I have had people say things to me like, "You have lived a charmed life" and "You are truly an inspiration."

You will notice as you read that even though I traveled alone, I was never really alone. Thanks to my mother and father, I learned early in life the importance of family, friends, and community—and I took it to heart.

I learned a number of other important lessons in my life as well—lessons that have helped me gain great friends, see the world, be successful in business, and enjoy each and every day. Along with my stories, I would like to share these lessons with you.

So without further ado, *sempre avanti* (Always forward)—from the prune ranch to skyscrapers!

CHAPTER 1

A SOLID FOUNDATION: OPTIMISM, RESOURCEFULNESS, AND FAITH IN GOD

I didn't realize we were in a Depression.

That's how it was when I was a boy in the 1930s. We didn't have much money, but we had good health, friends, good food, and a strong belief that the Good Lord would always provide. And you know what? He has! Read on and you'll see what I mean.

The Prune Ranch

Imagine my parents struggling to survive during the Great Depression and I am born, June 4, 1930!

My mother (Giuseppina) and father (Giuseppe) had immigrated to California from the island of Sicily—but not at the same time. Papa came to San Francisco from Trabia, Sicily, after the 1906 San Francisco earthquake, to join his brother Vincent. They lived with relatives on Alabama Street, and eventually saved enough money doing odd jobs to build flats in Bernal Heights. By then they had begun to work as peddlers, so the ground floor of the flats went all the way back to a barn for two horses they had, plus a wagon to carry the fruit and vegetables they sold in the neighborhoods.

Some years passed, and Uncle Vincent decided to seek his fortune in Santa Barbara. Papa sold the flats after converting the first floor to a grocery store, and collected mortgage payments. Then he moved to San Jose to be near his other brother, Sam, and his sister, Mary.

When Papa had bought a house in San Jose, he sent for my Mama to come to America to marry him. Mama was from the same Sicilian village, Trabia. When Mama arrived, she lived with her uncle in San Jose on a ranch, and Papa had to visit her there. Eventually they got married, and Papa then bought a ranch near my Mama's uncle, Turturici, and also next to the ranch of Mama's aunt, Lo Bono. Papa's brother Sam and sister, Mary, would visit often. So you see, all the relatives would get together and everybody spoke Sicilian, including myself. In fact, I was like a foreign student when I started grammar school!

1

Papa in San Francisco in the early 1900s,
before marrying my Mama.

I wasn't an only child. I have a sister, Marianna, who is eight years older than me, and a brother, Joe, who is four years younger. I remember when Joe was born. It was 1934, and I was staying at the Lo Bono ranch down the road during the delivery. To this day, I can still see my Papa—he was wearing a jacket with a sheep wool collar—as he arrived at the house to tell me I had *un fratello*!

The ranch we lived on was planted with prune trees. (This has afforded me lots of opportunities to make prune jokes. In 1980, I began a speech to the Rotary Club, "I was born in San Jose, California, on a prune ranch—and I have been *regular* ever since.")

My parents' wedding photograph, 1921.

I remember when Papa hired workers to pick his prune crop. When the prunes (or plums, at this point) start to dry on the tree, they begin falling to the ground. So to harvest them, we would shake the tree to make them all fall. It was hard work to handpick the crop, since it meant bending over for long periods to pick them up off the ground.

My Mama would put the prunes in sacks to be sold—she was great at sewing the sacks. (In fact, she used this skill later when she worked for the Golden Grain

Company in San Francisco, sewing sacks for the macaroni. Back then it was a small company, and she worked for the original owners. Sometimes they would even give her a ride home!)

My family would also work processing crops at other ranches. My sister, Marianna, tells me that when I was a baby they would put me in a wicker basket and take me to the different ranches while they packed boxes with apricots and cherries. They could earn extra money that way—this was the Depression, and they worked hard to put food on the table!

One day when my sister was around nine years old, she got a chance to pack *large* apricots, which was a great opportunity. You see, they got paid by the box, and she could have filled boxes more quickly because of the large apricots. But I kept starting to cry, and she had to keep stopping to console me, so she couldn't earn much at all. So I *owe* my sister!

Money was hard to come by then. Often, my sister didn't have new clothes for school, and her teacher would give Marianna some clothes from her family. In addition, Marianna received welfare coupons to buy shoes. She had to pick only certain shoes for welfare recipients, but she was happy to get new loafers.

On the ranch, Mama used to cook on a wood stove with wood chopped by my father. She used to wash clothes on a washing board (at night many times!), and would hang the clothes outside for the sun to dry. There was no washing machine or dryer! And I remember having to go out to the outhouse, since we didn't have a bathroom indoors. We did have an icebox. The iceman would come from the icehouse to bring us a huge block of ice, which would keep the box cool.

My Papa had a horse to plow the field for potatoes and tomatoes, and Mama used to make the best tomato paste. People would come to the ranch to buy it! Mama also baked wonderful bread in the outdoor oven Papa had built for her. Our relatives helped him build it, and they also pitched in to dig the "cellar" under our house—just a dirt floor and walls that made a cool enough place to store the wonderful preserves that Mama made. She would preserve peaches, olives, and Bing cherries with brandy. Papa and Mama would also make wine, root beer, beer, and ice cream, and they salted anchovies in a crock and preserved eggs, too.

We raised chickens and rabbits, and I would go with Papa to gather the warm eggs in the hen house. Papa would take an egg (still warm), poke a hole, then swallow! He said it made him strong—he would also put an egg in a glass of wine on occasion.

We also had a goat for milk, and Papa would gather mushrooms and mustard greens (*colucci* in Sicilian) from the ranch. We lived off the land!

Our family on the prune ranch: Mama, Marianna, and Papa in back;
in front are Joe (left) and me.

We ate a lot of chicken, rabbit, vegetables that they raised on the ranch, and pasta with tomato sauce and with vegetables. We actually didn't have much meat. Sometimes Mama would make meatless meatballs with cheese, breadcrumbs, and seasonings. She cooked them in her wonderful sweet tomato sauce. They were so good we almost preferred them to the ones with meat!

On occasion, we also ate snails in a wonderful tomato sauce. The snails were there on the ranch, and my parents would put them in a big bucket to clean them thoroughly. They were a treat! We used to like tripe in tomato sauce, too. And remember, my Mama would bake that wonderful bread. As a real treat she would take the hot loaf out of the oven and slice it in half, then add olive oil and Parmesan cheese. Marvelous!

Now and then Sam Conjulusa, a favorite "relative" who worked at a meat packing plant, would visit and bring us a huge bologna. It was so big my parents would put it in the bathtub to keep it cool. Later they would cut it into smaller sections for the icebox for refrigeration. And I remember Sam Conjulusa always gave me a fifty-cent coin. It was a lot of money back in the 1930s!

When people would visit us at the ranch, my parents would ask me to take them out to the tomato section and help them pick some to take home. My parents were generous! I knew where the good ones were and I would personally fill their bags. Then I would wash my hands after picking the tomatoes—the soap-suds would turn green.

Sunday was like a big Sicilian festival at our ranch. Friends and relatives gathered around a big outdoor table and ate and drank to their heart's content. Like I said, I didn't realize we were in a Depression!

We would go into town (San Jose) for weddings and receptions with music and singing and dancing. At an early age, when I was only about four or five, people used to ask me to tell a story that Papa had taught me. So, in Sicilian, I would tell stories that Papa had told me on his knee. They would put a chair in the middle of the room and everybody lined up against the walls to hear. I was "on stage" early in life! And I never forgot the Sicilian language. As you will see, it has helped me all my life.

We used to have two dogs on the ranch. One was a Collie named Spot, and believe me, he looked like Lassie. He was smart. Our ranch was at the end of this dirt road off of Meridian Road in San Jose. (This dirt road is now Blackford Lane, and our ranch is Blackford High School.) When my Papa had to go to town it left my Mama alone. Spot was very protective. He would sit on the road and look for anybody coming down it. He had two distinctive barks: one for strangers and one to notify Mama that Papa was returning.

Unfortunately, Spot disappeared one day, and Papa found him dead near the creek that was next to our ranch. Somebody had shot him! I'm sure he was shot by someone trying to enter our property to do harm.

Our whole family was brought to tears! Papa wanted me to have another dog to play with, so he got a smaller dog that I named Jimmy. I loved him so much. We used to run all over the ranch. He was so playful!

One day he disappeared, too. Papa and I got into the truck and drove all over the ranch and down the ranch roads, but we couldn't find him. He was such a friendly dog; we figured he was stolen by someone.

You learn a lot of lessons about life when you grow up on a ranch—hard lessons, and happy ones, too.

One day Papa took me with him in the truck loaded with potatoes to the potato chip factory. Oh, it was great! I remember helping to pick the potatoes—what an educational treat, to learn how potatoes grow. The truck we rode in was a Ford, and when we arrived at the factory the owner took Papa and me on a tour to see how they made potato chips. What a marvelous aroma! The owner gave me a large bag of warm potato chips to eat in the truck on the way back to the ranch. There I was: sitting in the truck with my Papa, eating warm potato chips. I was in heaven.

Then there was the time my parents had prunes out drying in large trays, and it started to storm. Mama, Papa, and my sister, Marianna, ran out to bring the prunes into the barn while the rain poured. I was watching from the window, and suddenly a bolt of lightning struck the ground right next to my sister! I thought, please God, help them! And I felt God answered by stopping the lightning and sparing my sister any harm.

As a young child I was taught by my parents to pray with all my heart. When I was about three years old, I would sit on my Papa's knees and he would tell me these wonderful stories. These stories were not of Jack and Jill, but of Jesus. As I sat listening, for example, he would tell this story:

One day as Jesus was wandering from village to village with his followers, they came to a hill. Everyone was tired, for they had been walking for hours. But Jesus said that he wanted them to pick up a stone and carry it to the top of the hill!

There was some grumbling among the followers, who said, "We are tired, and he wants us to carry a stone!" However, despite the many objections, all but one carried a large stone to the top of the hill. This one follower said to himself, "I'll bring these pebbles to the top, since they are small and very light."

When all of them arrived at the top of the hill, Jesus instructed them to sit on their stone. All of them were happy to sit and rest for a while. But the man who had carried the pebbles was still grumbling. He said, "I can't sit on these pebbles. They are too small!"

Then what happened was amazing. The followers felt something very warm underneath them and jumped up.

"Oh, how wonderful!" they cried. Jesus had turned the stones into hot bread! They feasted on their loaves of bread. But now the man who had brought pebbles had only crumbs to eat.

He rushed to Jesus and said, "Why didn't you tell me you were going to turn the stones into bread?"

Jesus said, "I'm testing your faith. Trust in me!"

The other story my Papa told me was about a young man who was in the main street of his village when he spotted an old man sitting on the side of the street. The old man was obviously in need of water. The young man gave him water from his flask, and the old man looked at him with these beautiful eyes and thanked him.

Many, many years later this young man died and went to heaven to face Jesus! Jesus said, "Have you lived a good life and helped others in need?"

"I have tried to be good and helpful," replied the man.

Jesus responded, "I know you have been good. Look into my eyes, and you will remember you gave me water. Enter the Kingdom of Heaven!"

My Mama also taught me to pray to Jesus and have faith. She said, "*Chi tiene fede a Dio non perische mai.*" This means "He who has faith in God shall never perish." This expression is very special to me, and I repeat it every day.

We lived on the prune ranch for most of the 1930s, but God soon had other plans for us.

One day Mama and Papa had to go to San Francisco to meet their lawyer. It turns out that the people who were making payments on the store and flats in San Francisco had moved out and abandoned their store equipment and supplies.

Papa brought back the meat slicer from the store, and had it in the back of the truck. When he arrived at the ranch, he picked it up to put it in the cellar. The blade was not secured, and it turned and cut off the tips of two fingers!

I will never forget how the blood gushed forth. My Mama got sheets and towels to tie off his arm and reduce the bleeding. My sister ran to one of our relatives down the road for help, and Papa went to a hospital in San Jose. They couldn't attach the tips of his fingers, so Papa said, "I want to keep them."

The doctor put them in a bottle with a preservative, and Papa stored them in the cellar. Sometimes when people visited us (and after sharing a few glasses of wine …), he would bring them down to the cellar to show off his fingertips! Thinking back now, they would have been useful during Halloween.

During the Depression my parents were getting something less than one cent a pound for prunes. They both worked in canneries in San Jose to try to supplement that income. But when the people abandoned the flats and store in San Francisco and defaulted on their mortgage payments to my Papa, my parents couldn't make the mortgage payments on the ranch. They did, however, now own the property in San Francisco again, so they decided it would be best to move to the flats. So, in 1937 my parents packed a few belongings, and we drove to San Francisco in our Model A Ford to start a new life!

Left: Marianna standing near the clothesline on the ranch.
Right: Joe and me in San Francisco.
The placard in the car window says "Roosevelt"!

San Francisco: Life on the Hill

Our flats in San Francisco were located at 205½, 206, and 207 Banks Street. To our west was Mission Street, to our east, Bayshore Boulevard, to our south, Alemany Boulevard, and just north of us was Bernal Heights Hill, or "the Hill" to us. The neighborhood today is called Bernal Heights.

The main corridor in Bernal Heights was Cortland Avenue, where you could find shops, a church, a movie house, and so on. Back then, the district was served by streetcar No. 9, which ran along Cortland Avenue to a point where the street went sharply downhill. The streetcar would reverse the chair backs for the trip toward Mission Street and along Mission all the way to First Street, stopping at the Key System terminal. (The Key System was a train system that ran on the bottom of the Bay Bridge to the East Bay.)

When we first moved in, there was a great street fair celebrating the opening of the library on Cortland Avenue. Mayor Angelo Rossi had secured backing to build this modern library, and behind the library were a playground and a gym.

The ground floor of the flats we moved into had been used as a grocery store, and there were two flats side by side on the upper floor. We took one of the apartments on the top. Later, Mama and Papa went to the Bank of Italy in North Beach (later renamed the Bank of America) to get a loan to remodel the store into a residential apartment. They then rented the two other apartments.

Top Left: Papa in the backyard of our Banks Street flats.
Top Right: Mama in our new kitchen.
Bottom: From left to right in the backyard: Papa; me; Joe;
my sister's husband, Pete Crosetti; Marianna;
my brother's godmother, Mrs. Rossi; and her two daughters.

Soon after we moved in, my sister brought me to Paul Revere Grammar School, close to Alemany Boulevard, to enroll me. It was then, I remember, I told her that I wanted to be called John. My real name was Mariano, a family name. (It is traditional in Sicilian culture to name the first son after the paternal grandfather.) But I wanted an American-sounding name.

The Paul Revere Grammar School graduation program, 1944.

I loved going to school to learn new things, and especially being in a big city and meeting children from different backgrounds. We used to walk to school. In fact, we used to walk home for lunch, where we sometimes had Campbell's soup.

One week we had a science project to collect pollywogs. Mrs. Nielsen, the eighth-grade science teacher, was impressed when Paul McKowen (a friend in the same class) and I presented her with a Mason jar filled with pollywogs. Paul and I had done something like Tom Sawyer and Huckleberry Finn: we had built a raft and floated over the swamp land near Alemany Boulevard. Yes, *swamp land* that today is the site of a popular farmers' market!

Paul Revere teachers were so dedicated. They took a real interest in us and also in our families. For instance, Miss Mildred C. Cavanagh took a special interest in me and taught me to write beautiful letters. She was a great influence on me and motivated me to attend the University of California in Berkeley. She also used to talk to my Mama and tell her that I should go to college. I sent her a Christmas card every year she was alive, and she in turn would send me one with encouraging words and inspiration!

I attended grammar school during World War II (1941–43). I still have a copy of the *Paul Revere Dispatch* from June 1943. There is an article on rationing, and headlines like "Plant for Victory" and "Buy Stamps and Bonds." We were issued stamps for coffee and meat during the rationing.

During the war the city put a siren on the top of Bernal Heights Hill, so if we were being attacked we could be warned in advance. Now and then the siren would blare during a test. We had blackouts—all the lights had to be out at night—and block wardens would patrol at night to make sure they were all out. We were told to look at the skies and report any unusual planes. We were even given pictures of our United States airplanes so we would know the difference. We lived with the fear that perhaps we would be bombed, so we all had to participate to keep our country free and safe!

We liked our new home. Our neighborhood—Cortland Avenue in particular—was like a village. Everybody would talk to each other. Back in the thirties and forties, we didn't have television!

Many of the shops on Cortland Avenue were mom-and-pop stores. The shop owners usually owned the building, living on the top floor and operating a business on the bottom. Examples were the small grocery stores, bakeries, barbers, the fish market, and the coal store. In those days a lot of people used coal for heating and cooking. The "Coal Man" used to sit in front of his garage (his coal storage) and watch the world pass by. He knew us all and saw us grow up. His wife would join him and do some knitting. Friends would join them—they always had extra chairs. It was a peaceful time!

Mama and Papa would shop at the butcher shops, bakery, and grocery stores, and buy fish from Mr. Frank's Fish Shop. Mr. Frank would have a huge pot on the sidewalk in front of his store and cook fresh crabs. Oh, they were wonderful. Mama would order three *live* crabs to make crab cioppino. Mama's sauce was outstanding, and then as a bonus she would put it on pasta. You haven't lived until you have pasta with crab sauce!

Food was at the center of our lives. Everything was fresh: the fish, the vegetables, fruit, eggs, and more. Mama and Papa used to walk to the farmers' market and buy direct from the growers, and Papa would put a huge box on his shoulders and climb up the steep hills to bring the fresh produce to our table.

In the 1930s, the milkman made home deliveries and left the milk behind the front door—it was safe! It was stored in glass bottles, which would be recycled. We loved to lick the cream off the bottom of the cardboard cap. We would flip the caps (head or tails), and collect them also.

I remember sometimes going to Jack's grocery store, located at the end of the No. 9 streetcar line, to get fresh milk. Jack had the "freshest" milk—Marin Dell was the brand. Also, I would buy large bottles of cream soda, strawberry soda, orange soda, and root beer on Sundays. In those days, Jack would get the items himself—self-serve came later. He used a long pole with a gripper to get products from the top shelves. There weren't any scanners, either. Jack would add up the prices the old-fashioned way: using his head.

We also would go to the All American Meat Market on Cortland, which was run by Mr. Battaglia. He was a wonderful friend to everybody. If you needed anything, he could help. The shop had sawdust on the floor to absorb any water or moisture. He used to give me a free hot dog from the case, and I would eat it right there and then. It was a delicious raw beef hot dog—still cold. My Mama would ask Mr. Battaglia to save the pork skin for her to make stuffed rolls. He would never charge her. Those were the days!

Our Catholic Church was St. Kevin's, located right on Cortland Avenue. My brother and I made our First Communion and Confirmation there. I used to love to go listen to the Sister tell stories of Jesus, and I greatly admired a life-size poster of St. Michael, with beautiful wings and a sword, fighting the bad angels. I admired him so much that I selected Michael as my middle name for Confirmation.

In catechism, the Sister used to give me small stars because I used to get all the questions correct on the tests. One day she said, "I don't have any more stars to give to John, so I want him to have this cross from my robe." I cherish this cross every day. I have it above my desk alongside a printed card that reads, "God is Greater than any problem I have."

St. Kevin's Church had a large hall underneath that was used for classes, festivals, and bingo. The festivals were especially happy events, with neighbors and people from other neighborhoods enjoying the fun activities. My father once bought a ticket for the grand drawing of $250, and he won! What joy, because we really needed the money.

Our neighborhood had many laborers, carpenters, electricians, plumbers, cement workers—a lot of union workers. My Papa joined the AFL-CIO laborers union and would go to the union hall to get jobs, such as digging ditches for construction sites. Papa was very strong and would take any job to put food on the table. For example, he worked for the federal Works Progress Administration (WPA) to clear forest area and worked on various WPA projects, mostly construction as a laborer.

Before joining the union, Papa had tried to make a living selling fruits and vegetables by truck—only he didn't have a truck, he had a Model A Ford. Papa and Battaglia (a relative—not the butcher) converted the Model A Ford to a truck right in front of our house on Banks Street. They cut off the rear of the Model A, and built sections on the rear with room for the various boxes of vegetables and fruits.

I used to go with my Papa to the different neighborhoods, such as Pacific Heights, and the cooks and other people would come out to buy the freshest of produce from "Joe" (my Papa). Also, Papa would fill a galvanized bucket with oranges or apples and I would go door to door to sell it for fifty cents. Then I would run back to give Papa the fifty cents and get another refill and sell some more. It was fun, and Papa was proud.

One time Papa asked me if I would like to go with him to the farmers' market to buy his inventory of fruits and vegetables for the day. We had to be at the market early—like 5:00 in the morning. What a thrill! Papa introduced me to the vendors and I saw him in action as he negotiated the best price.

There was one week when Papa netted only $7 because he had to buy a new battery for the truck. That was when it became necessary to give up being a peddler and to work as a laborer and join the union.

Later in life, Papa worked for the San Francisco Housing Authority as a gardener, at Hunters Point Housing Project. He worked until he was sixty-eight years old and had to retire. The pension was very little and there were no health benefits—there was no Medicare at that time. Believe me, these were tough times!

During the 1950s, Mama and my sister, Marianna, worked for the Rich Pie Shop. Rich Pie made quality pies and sold them to restaurants and coffee shops. They were the best! I remember we personally enjoyed a lot of pies: apple, pumpkin, berry, custard, lemon, and more. You see, Walter, the Chief Baker in charge, used to give Mama free pies to "bring home to the kids." (Walter would "accidentally" put his large thumb on a portion of crust and then claim it as damaged.)

Mama and Marianna would take the streetcar or bus very early in the morning to arrive at work by 4:30 AM; at work they would cut the fresh fruit for the pie fillings. Sometimes on the streetcar or bus going home, Mama would give away a pie to someone she was sitting with. In reality, Mama was promoting Rich Pie Shop—imagine the wonderful aroma of a warm apple pie made with cinnamon! She really earned those pies.

Top: Papa on the site of a public works project.
Bottom: Mama and Papa with our first TV,
which my brother, Joe, bought in the mid-1950s.

As I said, we didn't have television when I was growing up. But we did sit on the floor and listen to our favorite radio programs. We listened to *Little Orphan Annie* (Ovaltine was the sponsor), the *Lone Ranger, The Aldrich Family* ("Henry, Henry Aldrich!"), *Jack Armstrong (The All American Boy)*, Jack Benny, *Captain Midnight, Inner Sanctum,* and *The Shadow* ("Only the Shadow knows"). *Batman and Robin* was also popular. We used to send in Ovaltine caps to get the magic dog whistle that only dogs could hear. Also, we sent in for the *Captain Midnight* magic rings that would shine in the dark and allow us to decode messages.

We would go to the movie house on Saturdays and Sundays in the afternoon. For ten cents we would see two feature films (with stars like Gene Autry, the Lone Ranger, Hopalong Cassidy, and Roy Rogers) after viewing Movietone news and a serial film such as Buck Rogers, which we had to see on a "continued until next time" basis. My brother and I would buy one bag of popcorn (we couldn't afford two) and agree not to start eating until the movie started. But imagine having that warm bag of freshly popped popcorn under your nose! Soon we would break down and agree to have just one kernel....

Sometimes Mama would make us a bag lunch so we could eat it during the movie. The ticket seller in the booth wanted to know what we had in the bag. But she knew our Mama and allowed us to eat our lunch during the show.

After the movie we would play out scenes from it in our street. We used to go to the movies with our friends, so we had plenty of "actors" available. We would sleep really well because we were so tired from running around so much. At night Mama would tuck us in. I can still remember that gentle tug on the blanket. That was love!

Mama and my sister would go to the movies at night with friends, not only to enjoy what was playing but to get the free gift! I still have dishes that Mama got back in the forties and fifties. My Papa would go at night sometimes when they had prize drawings for bags of groceries. Papa even won a couple of times. In fact, he won at the New Cortland and the Lyceum Theatre on Mission Street. Papa would go to the movies during the day, especially for the cowboy episodes—he loved the Lone Ranger.

For fun, my brother, Joe, and I used to climb to the top of Bernal Heights Hill, which was also known as Nanny Goat Hill. (People actually used to raise goats on the slopes of the hill.) At the top of the hill you could see for miles—to the bay, downtown, to the East Bay. It was a magnificent view!

Papa used to help us make kites, and we would go to the top of the hill where it was windy and fly them. And it didn't cost anything. We didn't buy toys. We made our own!

Bernal Heights' residential area has many hills, and at that time empty lots with grass. We used to have grass fights, and we'd slide down the grassy slopes on a piece of cardboard. We even made a wonderful "coaster."

Our version of a racecar was built with boards and a wooden box for the hood. We would get ball bearings for the four wheels, and then a steering wheel from a car and attach it to a broomstick. With a clothesline rope we would attach it so that we could turn the front wheels. (And you didn't need a license to drive it!) I still remember my brother going down Cortland Avenue all the way to Bayshore Boulevard.

We did buy roller skates—the only toys we ever bought. The roller skates required a special key to tighten them to our shoes. A collector's item today! Again, we took advantage of the hills and roller-skated down some really steep streets. My brother was quite a daredevil, and he would come *straight* down! Unfortunately, he once fell head first and cracked his chin. He needed stitches, but it didn't slow him down.

Our childhood was marvelous! We used to play touch football in front of our house on the street. We played basketball, too. My brother was something of a free throw expert. He won a trophy! We also used to play "Hide and Seek," "One Foot off the Gutter," and "Kick the Can." We played marbles and had competitions. We collected comic books (*Superman, Captain Marvel, Batman, Archie,* etc.), and we used to trade them. I wish we had kept them!

Our Banks Street flats.

Top: Neighborhood kids playing football in the street, with Joe as quarterback.
Bottom: Joe (in front) and me (in back) with some of the kids
we used to play with—it was a multicultural neighborhood!

We were always running. Once I ran down a grassy empty lot and fell face down, and my hands hit some broken glass. My right hand was cut deep. Al Hemphill (one of our tenants in the flats, and a retired pharmacist) put iodine on the cut (Ouch!) and bandaged it well to stop the bleeding. To this day I have a crescent-shaped scar.

During the summer months the neighbors and Mama and Papa would put chairs in front of the house on the sidewalk and watch us play.

Once there was a bully who wanted to fight with me. I fought back and was winning! But then the father of the bully started to chase me. To my surprise, my Papa caught hold of the man and *lifted* him and said, "Don't you ever touch my son!" I was so proud of my Papa for defending me. And Papa was proud that I took on the bully even though he was bigger!

We would sit on the sidewalk outside of the house and look up to the sky. We would stare upward and wonder how far it goes. Is there a shell? Or are we looking at the bellybutton of God? He is so large we can't see him—or are we inside God?

My brother and I had read a book called *Poppy Ott's Seven League Stilts.* Inspired by the book, we built a pair of stilts and charged one penny to use them to cross the street in front of our house. We were entrepreneurs at an early age!

We also founded the Red Eagle Club down in our basement to hold meetings. It was there we planned our activities during the summer.

Mama and Papa wanted us to enjoy our summer and would take us to the beach at the Pacific Ocean. We would go to the Fleishhacker Zoo and to Playland-at-the-Beach, which had games, rides, a fun house with the famous Laffing Sal, and a merry-go-round. The merry-go-round had the brass ring—you had to lean from your ride and try to grab the ring, which was good for a free ride. I got it once!

"The beach" was located at the famous Cliff House, which had restaurants and beautiful views of the Pacific Ocean and the Seal Rocks. Sutro Baths nearby was popular for swimming—my brother and I were given woolen bathing suits, and the pools had different temperatures. Later, the Sutro Baths were converted to an ice rink, where I used to go for ice-skating.

I learned to swim in the Fleishhacker Pool: the world's largest outdoor saltwater swimming pool. This pool was famous for its high-diving board. The famous Tarzan (Johnny Weissmuller) used to dive and swim there!

Since Fleishhacker Pool was filled with saltwater, it was easy to swim and float. But when I had to pass the swimming test—a high school requirement—I took the test near our high school at the Young Men's Institute (YMI) pool, which was a freshwater pool.

I almost drowned! I was supposed to jump in at the deep end and swim to the shallow end, then swim back to the deep end. But I couldn't raise my arms! I quickly became exhausted because I was used to the saltwater at Fleishhacker Pool. I actually went down, and the lifeguard had to take a hook and pull me out. But I had kept my mouth closed, so I was okay. The Good Lord saved me!

Later on I learned to swim in freshwater, and passed the test at the YMI.

Now and then Mama and Papa would take us on trips outside of the city, too. My family would often take the "Daylight Train" to San Jose and Santa Barbara to visit our relatives. You may recall that Papa's brother, Uncle Vincent, had moved to Santa Barbara in the early 1900s. Well, he had invested in real estate in downtown Santa Barbara, and had become quite wealthy! We would stay for a week there—*beautiful* Santa Barbara. And in San Jose we would have many glorious reunion parties with Papa's sister and his brother and other friends.

Top Left: My uncle Vincent and Papa in Santa Barbara.
Top Right: Papa and Mama on one of our visits to Uncle Vincent's.
Bottom: The grand Santa Barbara Mission.

In 1939 my family went to the World's Fair in San Francisco. The city actually created Treasure Island in the San Francisco Bay, specifically for the World's Fair. We took the ferry boat to and from the fair. What excitement! There were people from all over the world. I was nine years old, and it made a great impression on me: the buildings, the statues, the flowers, and the people. My parents knew this would be a lifetime experience, so they sacrificed to bring us this adventure.

Exhibits at the 1939 World's Fair, staged on Treasure Island near San Francisco.

While we were growing up in San Francisco, Mama and Papa attended classes to prepare for their citizenship examination. Soon they had both earned their citizenship papers. I was so proud of them!

Al and Bell Hemphill were tenants in our flats, and Bell helped Mama learn to speak English. They would have coffee together and Bell would say, "This is a cup" and "This is a dish." Al was a retired pharmacist, and he used to love to talk to my brother, Joe. They would have tea together. Al once brought home a scooter for my brother, and Joe loved it. Wonderful people!

Our flats were also home to people who came to California from Oklahoma to work in the Henry Kaiser shipyards. (Interesting, since I would work for Henry Kaiser later on.) The shipyards were building Liberty Ships, Victory Cargo Ships, troop transports, and so on during World War II. So Henry Kaiser played a key role in the success of winning the war.

One of my relatives, Georgette Lo Bono, lived with us with her daughter, Linda. Georgette was a "Rosie the Riveter" and worked to build the ships during the war. Her husband was stationed in the Bay Area.

Another relative from Santa Barbara, Aileen Rubino, married to my cousin John Rubino, also lived with us for a while, while John was stationed in the Bay Area.

Another tenant, the Romano family, played an important role in my sister's life. Steve Romano dated my sister and married her before leaving for basic training at Camp Roberts in Southern California. He would have been sent to fight the war, but he became ill with pneumonia during training, and died.

Mama and Marianna took a train to Camp Roberts to return with his casket. It was so sad! I cried and cried—he was such a great guy. He had planned to become a building contractor after the war and build a home for my sister. He is buried at Golden Gate Military Cemetery in San Bruno, California.

Steve's younger brother, Joe, and I were close in age, and we were buddies. He wanted to go to college but was poor, so he wanted to make some money. He built a shoe shine box and would go down to Mission Street (then a busy commercial area) and shine shoes for ten cents. I would sometimes go with him to keep him company and talk about how someday we would go to college. And what do you suppose happened? Joe went to San Francisco State and became a schoolteacher. And me? I had quite a future in store myself.

Practice 1

Write down an important goal of yours. Next, brainstorm five to ten different steps that can take you closer to your goal—keeping in mind that resourcefulness pays off, and also that the Lord helps those who help themselves!

CHAPTER 2

VISUALIZE YOUR GOALS: IT WORKS!

You've heard people talk about the power of positive thinking, right?

I can tell you from experience that positive thinking—as well as setting and *visualizing* goals—will get you everywhere. Visualization has been a constant theme for me, and I believe it has played a huge role in my successes in education, business, and life in general.

Visualizing from the Start

The war was still on when I graduated from Paul Revere Grammar School, February 1, 1944. I still have the graduation program, which lists me as Student Body President and notes that I received the American Legion Award. Paul McKowen, my classmate and fellow pollywog catcher, also got an award—I was proud for both of us!

I cannot say whether visualization helped me excel in grammar school, but it was in high school that I definitely began to visualize success.

In 1944 I enrolled at Commerce High School on Van Ness Avenue in San Francisco. I picked Commerce because of its business courses, such as accounting, typing, business machines, and business law—so that just in case I couldn't afford to go to college, I would be prepared to get a job in business. I was, however, motivated to go to college, and I studied very hard and achieved straight A's during my four years, with the exception of two B's in gym (I had injured myself during soccer, and for two semesters I couldn't do some of the exercises). Also, I received one B in typing. The typing teacher, Miss Liuzza, told the class that she wanted me to get a B to show that I didn't have to be perfect!

I played soccer for four years and ran cross-country on the track team, and I planned to play football in my last semester. However, I was elected Student Body President and couldn't play football because of my new responsibilities. I had earned points toward my "Block C" athletic letter, but now I would be shy by one semester for the total points. However, in the last football rally, the head coach, Mr. Lester, awarded me the Block C letter, saying I had earned it. What a great honor!

As Student Body President I used to plan the rallies with our head Yell Leader, John Macia. We would meet at my house and plan the entire event. I liked to have the rally build up to a crescendo. For instance, we would have the football players come down the aisle onto the stage. Once during a basketball rally, we had a basketball player throw the ball up to the balcony.

In June 1947, in connection with my student body leadership at school, I got to attend "California Boys' State" in Sacramento, California. This was a marvelous experience in government, sponsored by the American Legion.

My high school photograph.
Don't miss the hair—that wave was natural!

I graduated January 26, 1948—the top honor student in my class, and Valedictorian for the graduation ceremony.

You see, I actually *visualized* at the beginning of high school that I was going to get straight A's, that I was going to be Valedictorian and Student Body President, and that I would lead the class down the aisle at graduation. I visualized the details:

even the music playing, and my name being announced as the top honor student and the Student Body President.

My graduation speech was entitled "UNESCO, Realization of Plato's Dream"—a timely topic since the United Nations was organized at the San Francisco Opera House while I was in school.

Mama and Papa threw a graduation party for me, and our relatives from San Jose came. My sister, Marianna, bought me a desk, because she always felt sorry for me studying on the kitchen table. She paid for the desk on a weekly basis. And it turns out I would definitely need a place to study going forward!

Earlier in the year, the principal at Commerce, Ralph Lehman, had recommended that I apply for a $2,000 Kiwanis Club college scholarship, which I did. When I was interviewed by the Kiwanis Club scholarship committee, Eugene Lorton, the chairman, asked me, "If you don't get this scholarship, will you still go to college?"

"Yes!" I emphatically replied. "I will work, I will sacrifice, I am determined!"

You see, I had promised my parents I would get an education—otherwise, their sacrifices would have been in vain. As I was growing up, I didn't realize we were poor. We had love, and somehow with the grace of God my parents provided. They stretched what they had—never complaining. I remember watching my Papa put cardboard in his shoes to cover the holes in his soles, and putting on heels from older shoes. My father would use my *used* razor blades. And Mama would reverse the collars in my old shirts.

I will always remember that phone call in 1947, just days before Christmas. Mr. Lorton was calling to tell me that I was one of the five students selected for the four-year scholarship. What a wonderful Christmas present! There were pictures of the five of us in the San Francisco papers.

Mr. Lorton told me I could go to any college I wanted. He recommended I go to Harvard. However, I explained that I had always planned to attend the University of California in Berkeley and commute with the Key System Train. I had visualized these details! Back in those days, the Key System terminal was at First and Mission streets in San Francisco. I had pictured myself taking the streetcar to the terminal, boarding the train to cross the Bay Bridge, getting off at Shattuck Avenue in Berkeley, and walking to my classes. And that's exactly what I did.

I received $50 per month for ten months each year, which added up to $500 for the year. I received the $500-per-year scholarship for the entire four years—$2,000 in total. As a recipient, I would each year address the Kiwanis Club membership at the Fairmont Hotel during a luncheon.

But I had to earn additional money as well. During the two months I was off during high school and college, I didn't go away for vacation, I worked and saved. In 1945 I was only fifteen years old, but it was still during the war and there was a shortage of men to employ. So, I was hired by the Railroad Commission to work at the State Building in the San Francisco Civic Center. My duties there included filing the Public Utilities cases (the Railroad Commission was renamed the Public Utilities Commission of the State of California, and its authority was expanded), as well as delivering mail to the different departments. Because I was friendly with everyone, it would take me longer than usual to deliver the mail. Fortunately, they wanted me back anyway! So I also worked there in the summers of 1946, 1948, and 1950.

In the years 1947 and 1949, the Commission did not get a budget for summer hires. In those years I would go job hunting by walking along Market Street and going to the employment offices of the companies located in the office buildings. In and out until I succeeded!

One year I walked into the National Shirt Shop on Market Street and got a job that very same day as a salesman.

Another summer I worked for Southern Pacific at the end of Market Street—near the Ferry Building. I had to punch a time card, and I was armed with a pellet pistol to protect myself from rats! My job was to get files from a warehouse, and oftentimes the rats would be hiding among the boxed files.

Another year I found a job with Barrango & Associates, a company that made mannequins for department stores. I would deliver the smaller mannequins on foot in the Union Square area. Of course, I would get a lot of people staring: the mannequins were nude! The company also made realistic heads for the mannequins—quite a work of art.

During Christmas I got a job with the Post Office, delivering packages from the back of military trucks. We would jump off and back on the truck, over and over, delivering packages in residential and commercial areas.

In February 1948 I began my life as a Berkeley college student. Going to the University of California had been my dream—as I said, I visualized attending! What a beautiful campus, and what great excitement! We had the Golden Bears football team, which went to the Rose Bowl three times while I was a UC student. Jackie Jensen was a hero—he was the Golden Boy. And Pappy Waldorf was the inspirational coach at the time.

My experience at Berkeley was in great contrast to my time at Commerce in downtown San Francisco. At Berkeley I attended classes in many different buildings. And, whereas at Commerce we had students from all over San Francisco, at the University of California in Berkeley, we had students from all over the world!

I wanted to get involved, but I wanted to get good grades—so I knew that I had to strike a balance between extracurricular activities and studying. The University of California was my opportunity to visualize.

During my first two years I achieved an A average and was inducted as a life member into Phi Eta Sigma, a scholastic honor society. I was then elected president of the organization, and in 1950 I got to attend the national convention in Texas. The *Daily Californian* (the University paper) reported this in the October 24, 1950, issue:

> **John Rubino Travels to Texas for Phi Eta Sigma Convention**
> John Rubino, delegate to the national convention of Phi Eta Sigma national scholastic fraternity will take a free ride to Texas. Rubino will leave tomorrow morning for Los Angeles, where he will take the Sunset Limited to San Antonio, Texas. While in San Antonio, Rubino hopes to visit the Alamo before going on to the University of Texas at Austin. At the convention the delegates will discuss the activities of their chapters during the past two years and elect their national officers, Rubino said. The convention, held October 27 and 28, will not concern itself only with scholastic activity, Rubino explained. There will also be a banquet at which T. S. Palmer, president of the University of Texas, will speak and a dance for the delegates. The delegates will be taken on a tour of Texas University and of Austin. Rubino will return to U.C. by the northern route of Southern Pacific.

A trip of a lifetime! I was twenty years old and traveling to Texas by train—the Sunset Limited. Plus, this was my first trip out of the State of California.

One evening on the train I decided to go to the club car. What excitement! There was a piano player entertaining the room, and a beautiful woman sitting on the piano. Everybody was having a great time. The woman on the piano (Did I mention she was beautiful?) got down and sat right next to me, and asked who I was and where I was going. I told her, and she said she was very proud of me and wished me good luck and gave me a kiss on my cheek. Then I asked about her plans. She replied that they were going to New Orleans to film a movie—*A Streetcar Named Desire.* Her name? Vivien Leigh!

When I arrived in San Antonio I got off to find a hotel room, but before that I went to use a restroom in the park across from the train station. For the first time in my life I saw a sign for a restroom that said "Colored." My heart fell!

I went on a tour of San Antonio and the Alamo, as I had planned. Along the Rio Grande in San Antonio there were restaurants and shops. One shop in particular showed a glass blower making different figurines, including one of a grand piano and bench. I bought it for Mama. She always loved it. I still have it on the mantle over the fireplace in my living room.

At the University of Texas we were assigned our rooms, and I shared mine with some Texas students. I will never forget how curious they were to know whether I attended the University of California with black students. I said yes, and that I have black friends. I told them that I went to a high school in San Francisco that had a student body that was 50 percent black.

When I returned to the UC campus, I reported back at our chapter meeting and recounted this attitude toward blacks. We were all dismayed and hoped that this attitude would change. I reported that as top students in a scholastic fraternity, we must do what we can in our lives to improve the situation. I was really getting an education!

Left: Visiting the Union at the University of Texas in Austin. Right: My college photo.

Don't Be Afraid to Ask

During my four years I was active on the campus even though I was a commuter; that is, I didn't live on or even near the campus. I couldn't live in a fraternity house—I really couldn't afford to belong to a fraternity. So, being an "independent," I could relate to the problems that presented themselves to students who didn't belong to a fraternity. For instance, we had no organized social activities and no meeting place. In addition, commuters who had cars had difficulty dropping off passengers—and for that matter picking them up—at Sather Gate. Peter Loret (a classmate) and I both recognized this problem, and I wondered what to do. The situation was not new—students had been dealing with it for years. So did I just decide to forget about it?

No! I decided to go to the top! I asked for a meeting with the president of the University of California, Robert G. Sproul. He was great: inviting me to his office and asking me how he could help the independent, or commuting, students. I related the social issues and the problem of loading and unloading passengers at Sather Gate, and asked about a space where we could hold meetings.

His response?

"Congratulations, Rubino, you made your case!"

We got all of our requests! Our new organization got publicity in the *Daily Californian,* and we called it the "Cal-Muters." We held dances, luncheons, and meetings to discuss whatever was on our mind. I was elected president of the Cal-Muters and became known as the voice of the independents. President Sproul was extremely happy with the results and appointed me to serve on his *Daily Californian* Advisory Board.

So don't be afraid to ask—and don't be afraid to go to the top, either. My brother, Joe, and I learned this lesson together, when I was in college and he was in high school.

The two of us had always wanted to change our address in San Francisco from 205½ Banks Street to 207 Banks Street. We felt that the "½" was embarrassing, plus, it was misleading and inaccurate to portray our flat as "½"—we were now living in the bottom flat, and it was the largest unit of the three!

So, we went as youngsters to City Hall in San Francisco to request that the flats be renumbered to 207, 209, and 211.

We made our case and obtained the proper forms and signatures—and we had to be good ambassadors. To obtain the necessary approvals, we had to convince some of our neighbors to change their addresses as well!

We were young, but we wanted to bring dignity to our family. We won approval from the city and our neighbors. Soon we could say, "We live at 207

Banks Street." We were so proud! And our parents were proud that we had learned to take charge at an early age.

I should mention that Joe also excelled in his own right—proof of our solid foundation! He attended Commerce High School four years after I did, and he also became Student Body President and earned a $2,000 Kiwanis Club scholarship. And Joe once made the papers in San Francisco when 120 delegates from nine public and thirteen parochial schools at a meeting at the City Hall elected him "Mayor for the Day" by popular vote. He got to spend the day in Mayor Elmer Robinson's office, and got his picture in the paper. Our family was so proud.

Joe as Mayor for the Day on April 21, 1952, shaking the hand of
Mayor Elmer Robinson.

Joe and I also had a lot of adventures together around this time. In 1951 I was twenty-one years old, and ready to buy a car. So my brother and I went to Van Ness Avenue ("Automobile Row") in San Francisco and shopped for one. I had saved $1,800, and I was able to purchase a beautiful used 1949 Mercury sedan with a stick shift. In particular, we were attracted to the chartreuse vinyl seat covers.

But are you ready for this? We didn't really know how to drive! And not only that: when the salesman drove the car to our house, he couldn't get it into the garage because the door was too narrow.

To solve the garage door problem, we decided to put in an overhead door, which gave us about 1½ inches on either side in the doorway. We had to be very careful when driving in and out, to say the least! However, once we solved the door problem, we had a new issue. Once the car was in the garage there was enough room to open the door and get out, but because of the tight fit near the garage opening, we couldn't walk out of the garage!

What to do? Well, the answer lay in the space underneath the stairway that led to the upstairs flat—the wall under this stairway separated the garage from the living room in the lower flat. Luckily at this point we were living in the lower flat. So, we had a carpenter come and cut into the wall under the stairs, creating a doorway into a closet in our living room. This meant that whenever we went for a drive, we would leave and return via the living room closet!

In 1951 we didn't have a car in the family, so the Mercury was a great family treat. And about that little problem of not knowing how to drive? I went to driver training classes and learned to drive with the stick shift, and with God's help I even passed my driver's test.

For much of the time that I was at UC Berkeley, I didn't have my own car. But I was fortunate to have a good friend at Cal by the name of Frank Torkelson. When our team went to the Rose Bowl, Frank drove me, Branny Yaich, and two others in his Chevrolet to Pasadena. And Cal went three times to the Rose Bowl, so we had a great journey each time! We got to see the game and also the Rose Bowl Parade.

One weekend Frank Torkelson got a small fishing boat and invited me and Eddie Salcedo to go fishing for striped bass on Frank's Tract in the Delta. Eddie, who worked at a bakery, brought hot rolls to make sandwiches, and we had cold cuts and beverages in an icebox. Well, we cast our lines out and sat there enjoying the hot rolls, but we *waited* and *waited*—no fish! We soon lost track of the time, and it started getting dark. All of a sudden a strong wind started to blow water into our boat, and we had to start bailing water out to keep from sinking! The river got rough, and we got worried: we were being tossed around, and we had to keep bailing water out. After a while we finally got the boat to shore. No fish, but we thanked God for keeping us safe!

During my later years at Berkeley, Frank would on many occasions give us a ride to the campus and let us off at Sather Gate. I was glad that with our Cal-Muters organization, he could now let us off without a hassle.

Top Left: Attending a Cal Bears game with Roland Quintero (middle) and Frank Torkelson (foreground). Top Right: Mama standing in the doorway of the newly renumbered 207 Banks Street! Bottom: Me with the fabulous Mercury.

Cars were very important to us because they allowed us to share with our friends and explore together. My good high school friend Roland Quintero and I used to drive to the Russian River for vacation. We would stay at his aunt's cabin in Guerneville, and go to dances there and in Rio Nido. It was great!

Roland and I also had quite a time when we drove to Lake Tahoe once during the winter. We stayed at a cabin with friends. While we were there, there was a terrific snow storm, and we couldn't get out! Finally, after a couple of days, the Highway Patrol led us out with the snowplow. We had our parents worried, but we survived! Actually, going *to* Tahoe was dangerous too: we couldn't see ahead of us because it was snowing so hard. We kept having to stop the car and very carefully check to see if we could proceed. Once, we banged the car into a snow bank. Luckily, we didn't go over!

One night, I got a call from Roland—we were all in bed. Roland said, "Let's go to Yosemite tonight." I had never been to Yosemite. How exciting! I went into my parents' bedroom and told them that Roland and I were leaving for Yosemite and not to worry.

It was a marvelous experience—it was during the spring. We saw waterfalls, flowers, deer, the beautiful mountains, and trees. It was magnificent! In those days, the road was very narrow, and you had to drive slowly in case a car was coming from the opposite direction. If one was, you had to get really close to one side of the road. We were young, free in spirit, and didn't even consider the danger!

In 1952, I was in my final year as an undergraduate at UC Berkeley. In addition to my Cal-Muters involvement and my position on the *Daily Californian* Advisory Board, I was appointed to the Activities Coordinating Board, and I was a member of the Honor Students Society, a member of the Store Board (for the Student Body Store), and a director of Men's Counseling. I had served as a counselor for many semesters.

One particular highlight was when I was inducted into the Order of the Golden Bear. I am a life member and I can attend the Order's meetings to this day. I served as a scribe at the time.

In addition, I was elected as a life member of Class Club '52 (an honor group selected on the basis of leadership on the campus). Plus, I loved taking Spanish, and because of my scholastic achievements in that language, I was asked to become a member of Alpha Mu Gamma, a foreign language honor society.

My undergraduate major was in business administration with an emphasis on accounting and marketing. I had intended to take the CPA (Certified Public Accountant) test at the end of my studies. However, that's not what happened.

I decided instead to graduate in June 1952 and go to Boalt Law School, thus continuing on at Berkeley as a graduate student. And, inasmuch as I was going to be a graduate student, my friends encouraged me to run for the student body office of Graduate Representative.

I really got into it in 1952, campaigning for the independent student. I brought my message to the electorate: that the Cal-Muters organization would be continued, to bring a sense of unity for all students. I even went to fraternities and sororities, and debated my opponents in front of Sather Gate. And guess what: I won the election! President Sproul congratulated me—on my election as Graduate Representative on the Executive Committee (ASUC).

Shortly after this, I was accepted into Boalt Law School. However, the admissions officer insisted that I resign my position as Grad Rep! I replied that I felt I could do both … but the law school was not convinced.

I contacted President Sproul and told him that I wished to defer entering Boalt and serve my term as Grad Rep. I also mentioned that, in the interests of doing as much as I could during my time as Grad Rep, I planned to enroll in the Graduate Business Administration program and get my MBA. President Sproul was pleased, saying that an MBA and law degree combination would be great training.

In fact, both of us thought it was a great plan. But what happened next was a shocker!

Practice 2

Take a moment to visualize yourself achieving the goal you wrote about in Practice 1 (or some other goal if you prefer). Visualize the details: how it will feel, how you'll be dressed, how you'll act, etc.

CHAPTER 3

TRUST THAT WHEN GOD CLOSES A DOOR, HE REALLY DOES OPEN A WINDOW (PART 1)

When we left off, I had just graduated from UC Berkeley, but had plans to get my MBA and then my law degree. I was still very involved with the university as Graduate Representative. In my mind, I was still a student. So neither I nor President Sproul could even have imagined what happened next.

Shocking News—and a Silver Lining

The shocker to me and President Sproul was that I got drafted!

In 1952 the Korean Conflict was going strong, and the military draft was active. As long as I was in school, I was supposed to be deferred. (I had taken ROTC for two years at UC Berkeley, and they wanted me to continue—but I didn't want to follow a military career.) However, I had just graduated and put my law school plans on hold, and had enrolled in the MBA program instead. Somehow, this change of plans had made me eligible for the draft! Apparently, law school would have been considered a continuation of my intended course of study, but the MBA was seen as extra study on top of the undergraduate degree I had completed—so I was no longer deferred.

After I received the draft notice, President Sproul wrote the Defense Department explaining that I was a leader and that if I was allowed to continue my studies I would later be of more assistance to the government. But the draft board in San Francisco insisted that by going for a master's degree I had opened myself up to be drafted—had I gone on to Boalt directly, I would have been deferred. President Sproul tried to convince the board members to change their minds, but to no avail.

President Sproul then arranged for me to request a direct officer commission in the Finance Corp. I went before a board of officers at the Presidio in San Francisco. They said I would get a commission ... if I could get my master's degree!

We went back to the draft board with this new information. But the draft board refused me the deferment so that I could get my master's. I was in a pickle!

President Sproul finally asked that I at least be sent to Officer's Candidate School. The draft board said that I had to be drafted and wait for orders to attend officer's school while I was in training for combat in Korea.

Needless to say, I did a lot of praying and visualizing that everything would work out according to God's plan.

I was inducted into the Army on December 6, 1952, with orders to report to Ford Ord near Monterey, California. This turn of events would have a tremendous influence on my whole life!

I would like to quote the Commanding General at Ford Ord, Major General R. B. McClure, from his message that appears in the yearbook I received after basic training:

> This book records a new and important period in your life—the time and effort given at Fort Ord in becoming a soldier in the United States Army.
>
> You have learned to adjust your activities so that you are an efficient, effective, and independent member of the Army team. You have set aside certain individual liberties and privileges, but you have assumed added responsibilities as a disciplined and trained fighting man ready and willing to defend your homeland.
>
> You have become a better man mentally, morally, and physically. You have found new friends that will stand by you throughout life, and you have acquired added prestige and honor as a loyal and patriotic American citizen.
>
> You arrived at Fort Ord as a civilian; you depart as a soldier and Infantryman. Walk proudly, for you are now responsible for the reputation, tradition, and history of the finest Army in the world and that Army's mightiest branch—the Infantry.
>
> I hope we will serve together again as soldiers, as Infantrymen, and defenders of our great Nation. Wherever you go, may you walk with God.

I am very proud that I served! The yearbook we were given is a memento of the many military activities and experiences we participated in while I was in basic training with E Company, 63rd Infantry Regiment, Fort Ord, from December 22, 1952, to April 11, 1953. It includes photos of us in company formation, standing in that old familiar line, swimming, learning to use automatic rifles, hand grenades, and the like, and has headlines such as "Field Mess: It tasted good after a hard morning's training," "Pay Day: A formation we never missed," "Bayonet: The close combat weapon," and "Shots: Somebody said that they use a square needle." These bring back memories!

Top: My buddy Frank Terranova scaling a wall in basic training. We were in shape!
Bottom: When I went into the service, I wanted my brother to use the Mercury. Here he
is with his future bride, Pat—they met at "Joe's Creamery" on Cortland Avenue!

One morning when we were in formation, Sergeant Faggett, our drill sergeant, asked if any of us could speak a foreign language. I stepped forward and told him that I could speak Italian, Sicilian, and Spanish. There were a few others who also could speak a foreign language. We were marched to a testing center located in the Classification and Assignment Center building.

Obviously, we all wanted to do well. The test, and I remember it well, started in the language! Therefore, you had to know when to start the exam—and it was fast. God was with me, because I passed as fluent in both Italian and Spanish. Dante Marcolina and Peter Armanini also passed the Italian test, and Ralph Weber passed the German exam.

We were interviewed by a counselor who indicated that there was a chance we would be sent to Europe as interpreters. However, we would still have to finish the four months of basic training, and we wouldn't find out until the end.

The suspense was too much. Now and then, Ralph Weber and I would go to the office and ask how we could better prepare ourselves to become interpreters … basically we were fishing for information: would we be sent to Korea to fight, or would we go to Europe instead? At one point the counselor told us that since we passed very high on the exams, we would not have to attend Monterey Language School—we were already prepared for the job of interpreter. This seemed like a good sign—it helped to know that we had passed high on the tests.

But the plot thickens! Shortly after I passed the foreign language tests, the Commanding Officer, First Lieutenant Karl Rettstatt, called me into his office to inform me that I had been accepted for officers training after basic training. Remember, officers training had been my goal! Now I didn't know whether to take officers training, or to turn it down in hopes of getting stationed in Europe instead. However, the C.O. was aware of my high marks on the language tests and told me that chances were good that I would be sent to Europe. So I mustered my faith and took the risk: I turned down officers training.

I was happy to learn that our Executive Officer, Second Lieutenant John McKnight, thought this was a good decision. McKnight was a sharp former Ranger, and I also respected his opinions.

I will never forget the morning when the Commanding Officer read the names of the soldiers who would be going to Europe. I was told that I would be going to Austria!

As soon as I heard the news, I ran to a phone booth to call home. My Mama started crying. I said, "Mama, I'm going to Austria, not Korea." She was relieved. I comforted her further by saying that on my first leave in Europe, I would visit our relatives in Trabia, Sicily. Mama was so happy!

Top Left: Ralph Weber at Ford Ord. Top Right: Dante Marcolina at Fort Ord.
Bottom: Playing a game of chicken during a break in basic training—that's
me with my boot out front.

Before we shipped out to our various destinations, we had a graduation ceremony with blue scarves and a parade. I invited my family to come. My brother, Joe, drove the Mercury to Monterey, and it was a glorious day!

Making the Best of a Good Situation

On April 24, 1953 (my Mama's birthday), those of us who would be stationed in Europe flew to Camp Kilmer, New Jersey, to await the ship, the *U.S.N.S. Geiger,* that would take us across the Atlantic.

In the meantime, we had from April 24 until around May 19 to enjoy the New York area. I was lucky to be with my good friends Dante Marcolina and Peter Armanini, so we could all go sightseeing together.

Before I embarked for Austria,
my Mama took me to lunch at Fisherman's Wharf and
bought me a military cap and special brass for my uniform.
Here I am wearing them in New York City.

Dante had relatives in Philadelphia and invited Pete and me to go to their home and have a delicious home-cooked meal: polenta and meatballs with tomato sauce. The polenta was placed in the middle of the table on a wooden board, and we used a paddle to put our share onto our dishes. Polenta is popular in Northern Italy but it's not a Sicilian dish, so I had never had it before—it was delicious! They also brought us to an Italian Club where we watched games of bocce ball. Another first for me was to go to a seafood restaurant in New Jersey and eat raw oysters. We liked them so much we ordered more.

While in New York, we stayed at the Diplomat Hotel, which was located at 108 West 43rd Street—just east of Broadway and Times Square. I have a postcard I had sent home that depicts the hotel. Dated May 3, 1953, it says, "Hi! This is a nice hotel. We have a radio in the room—free of charge. We are near everything. Love to all, Johnny."

I prepared a sightseeing tour of New York with Dante and Pete. We went to the Empire State Building, of course. On a postcard that I sent to my brother on May 5, 1953, I wrote: "Empire State Building, New York City—Fifth Avenue between 33rd and 34th streets. The tallest structure in the world. 102 stories high, it measures 1,472 feet to the tip of the TV tower. You feel like you are in a space ship up in the clouds. We went up the Statue of Liberty, too. Love to all, Johnny."

We walked up the circular stairs inside the Statue of Liberty and then looked out the windows at the crown. We had gotten to the island by ferry. What a thrill for us all!

We also visited Wall Street and Times Square, and went on a horse-drawn carriage ride through Central Park. The driver was Italian!

At night a tourist guide brought us to a "Dime a Dance" social club. We had to buy tickets for ten cents each, and each time we asked a girl to dance we had to give her a ticket after the music stopped. If we wanted to dance some more, we had to give her another ticket. We were not too happy with such a commercialized way of socializing. So, we went to dinner at a deli in Times Square and used our dimes for food instead!

On May 19, 1953, we boarded the *U.S.N.S. Geiger* for our exciting trip across the Atlantic Ocean. The *Geiger* was one of a globe-circling fleet of Navy and commercial ships operated under the Military Sea Transportation Services. This Navy agency provided ocean shipping for the United States Armed Forces.

I sent a picture postcard of the *Geiger* to Mama on May 26, 1953. I wrote the card in Italian, saying that we had already sailed for seven days and that I had been able to make the trip in good health. I also said that the next day we would stop in Casablanca, Africa.

On May 28, 1953, I wrote a postcard to my brother, Joe. It said, "Hello, Brother, I'm actually in Casablanca, Africa. I went on a 2½ hour tour by bus arranged by the boat with the sightseeing company. I never realized how the natives live here—I had to see it to believe it. The women actually wear veils in front of their faces. There are two distinct sections of town (where the natives live and the European section which is modernistic)."

On the tour, we learned about and even visited some extremely interesting places. I bought a goatskin billfold that was beautifully hand carved. However, I couldn't keep it because of the odor. It turns out that they use some kind of urine to cure the skin!

After Casablanca we sailed to Naples, Italy, for an overnight stay. We had to go through the Strait of Gibraltar; once we had, we entered the *calm* Mediterranean Sea.

Believe me, there were times when the Atlantic Ocean was really rough. One night I had guard duty on deck and the waves were so high that I had to hold on to a railing to keep from being tossed into the ocean. It was really pitch black, but I remember those huge waves!

In Naples we were allowed to go ashore. I asked about buying a cameo for my Mama, and one of the ship's crewmembers recommended "Michele Fannuccilli—The Best Art Works in Cameos—Coral—Tortoise Shell" (I still have the business card). We were warned not to buy cameos from street vendors because many times they were selling fakes.

I purchased a beautiful cameo for $75. I remember that the shop gave me a magnifying glass so that I could see the exquisite carving. My Mama cherished it!

I also visited a Catholic church to light a candle. As I was praying, the local priest came to me to pray for my safety. I was dressed in my military uniform. He blessed my mother's cameo and also gave me a small religious medal of our Blessed Mother Mary, which he also blessed. I have carried this medal in my wallet for over fifty years, next to my Mama's picture!

The next morning we sailed to Livorno (also called Leghorn), on Italy's west coast. Leghorn's Palazzo Grande, the 7617 USFA Support Command Headquarters, was at that time the nerve center of the U.S. Army's port of entry for Austria.

We were then transported by train to Austria, traveling up through Northern Italy. We stopped in Pisa, Florence, Bologna, and Trento. The countryside was absolutely beautiful! After Italy we passed the Alps, and finally we arrived in Linz, Austria.

On one of the nights after we arrived, we went to the Enlisted Men's Club at McCauley to celebrate my twenty-third birthday, June 4, 1953. I was very appreciative that my buddies—John Gazarella, Marco Ferrero, Pete Armanini, Dante Marcolina, and Frank Rizzi (all Italian interpreters like myself)—wanted to make sure I had a birthday celebration.

Once we had arrived in Austria, we were informed that although we would be interpreters as we had thought, we would also be assigned other duties. To be assigned these duties, I met with a WAC (Women's Army Corps) captain, who was marvelous. She read my background thoroughly, and then told me that a master sergeant stationed in Salzburg who had been assigned to the Inspector General as an Auditing Specialist was being rotated back to the States. She said my university background in accounting and business would qualify me for the job! However, I would have to be interviewed by the Inspector General, Colonel Murray McGowan, first. If he approved, I would be a member of the Inspector General team as an Auditing Specialist and as an Italian interpreter.

The next morning I was picked up by a captain in a brown Army sedan, and we drove to Salzburg to meet with the Inspector General. I was very anxious to make a good impression! You see, we had recently heard that there were actually too many Italian interpreters stationed in Austria, so I felt there was a chance I would end up getting shipped off to Korea after all, if for some reason I didn't land this job.

Upon entering the office of the Inspector General, I gave Colonel McGowan my best salute. Believe me, my suit was pressed, my shoes were sparkling, my brass was shining. He told me to be seated, and then looked over my folder for quite some time. When he noticed that I had attended the University of California in Berkeley, he mentioned that his daughter was at school there—then he said he wanted my opinion on something!

He opened a door on the right side of his desk and pulled out a bunch of letters. The problem, he said, was this: his daughter wanted to buy a car. He wanted to know, did I think that a car would be a good idea?

I replied that it would, because as a girl she would be attending fraternity parties, and if she wanted to leave for any reason she would be able to drive her car and not wait for somebody else to take her back to her quarters. In addition, at night it would be good to drive rather than walk alone.

He said that he liked my reasons and that he would grant her a car. Then he said, "And by the way, would you like to work for me?"

"Yes, sir!" I said. And so began my European adventure of a lifetime!

During my orientation for working for the Inspector General, I was given the *Handbook for Inspector General,* issued by the War Department Office of the Inspector General, Washington, D.C. (June 1947), along with some of the history of the Inspector General. I was also given *A Pocket Guide to Italy,* since I would serve as an Italian interpreter when needed. This was an excellent guide to Italy, but very importantly a guide to our behavior! In fact, a guide like this one should be given to all persons visiting overseas. The section titled "Some Things to Do and Not to Do" explains: "Remember you are a representative of the United States and an ambassador of good will." "Don't show off, boast, brag, or bluster." "Act toward Italians in their country as you would expect them to act toward you in yours." "Respect their customs and traditions, their churches and cathedrals." On page 1, the first paragraph states: "Whether you go to Italy on official duty or visit it on leave or liberty, while you are there you will be a sort of ambassador for your country. Probably you have heard a statement like this many times, but it cannot be repeated too often. Italians will judge the United States by you. They will watch you, listen to you, and say, 'So that is how Americans act and think, is it?'"

I was very proud to serve on the Inspector General's team. We truly respected each other for each team member's role. We had important responsibilities to perform, and each of us realized it. I was dedicated to serving with distinction and loyalty.

My tour of duty covered about eighteen months (1953–1954) in the Austrian Command. It was an experience that I will never forget and will treasure forever. Austria is a beautiful country and I was privileged to see it firsthand.

My activities revolved around our headquarters barracks in Camp Truscott, which was located along the Salzac River, and our offices in downtown Salzburg, located in a beautiful old building situated right on the Salzac River. The barracks were built by Hitler during World War II for his Special Troops. I was assigned my own room with hardwood floors.

To get to work each day, I would take a military bus to downtown Salzburg. I would get off a few blocks before the office and walk along the path next to the Salzac River to enjoy the beauty and see the Austrians going to work. Many Austrians used bicycles, and the young and old men and women traveled at a quick pace. And many of them wore colorful costumes! For instance, the men wore Lederhosen.

Our Mirabell Service Club (in Salzburg) and our Public Information Division did an excellent job of furnishing us with descriptions of the various festivals and customs we might witness during the holiday season. We felt that our welfare was considered and we were informed and made to feel at home away from home.

In addition, we were given wonderful brochures on how to enjoy our recreation time, complete with descriptions of the area and hotels available to us. For example, we received a booklet of historical and current information on beautiful Berchtesgaden, high up in the Alps, where the Army had established a Leave and Rest Center. We used to visit on weekends to relax in hotels that were built by Hitler, some for his troops, and one very swank one that was built for his favored guests.

Top: Me at the General Walker Hotel in Berchtesgaden, Germany, about 4,000 feet elevation. Bottom: On guard duty.

As part of my duties with the Inspector General as Auditing Specialist, I traveled extensively. Vienna was especially memorable, and we visited often. I was given an allowance to stay in a hotel and to dine out. It was marvelous to be able to stay in a first-class hotel for 26 schillings ($1) and eat in the hotel dining room for $1!

I wrote a letter on August 29, 1953, to a friend of mine in San Francisco to describe my experiences in Vienna. For example, I told her about five tours I went on during one two-week stay in the city: a city tour that included the Rathaus (city hall), plus tours of the Grinzing Wine District (much laughter and dancing and drinking!), Schöenbrunn Palace, Hofburg Palace, and the Vienna Woods. Also, at one point on the way to Vienna (in Enns, Austria), we had to travel through the Russian-controlled territory—that is, *behind the Iron Curtain*—for about 100 miles.

I visited various other towns in Austria, too, while working for the Inspector General. I remember in particular an assignment to St. Johann, Austria, in April of 1954. Even though it was spring, the snow on the ground was very deep—and being from the San Francisco Bay Area, I had only *limited* experience in dealing with snow, not to mention snow packs and the hidden dangers underneath.

One night after enjoying a great Austrian feast at a restaurant near my hotel, I decided to take a "shortcut" across a snow-covered field to return to the hotel. Bad idea! I set off across what looked like a big empty lot—and suddenly the snow gave way to reveal a very deep hole beneath my feet. But God was with me! There was a tall wooden pole right next to me and I grabbed it with both arms to stop going down any further into the unknown.

I knew that nobody was around to help, and that nobody would know I had fallen in. I prayed to God to help me! While still holding on to the pole for dear life, I put one foot forward onto what looked like solid snow. The snow under my foot felt *firm*. So I stretched ever so slowly with my leg—still firm! With a *burst of faith* I let go of the pole and started taking one foot at a time. I made it across alive! And I had learned a valuable lesson: You really don't know what lies below the snow.

One other work-related trip was really a highlight of my one and a half years tour with the Inspector General. Three officers and myself received travel orders to "WP Leghorn and Verona, Italy," in connection with IG activities on or about May 9, 1954, for approximately twenty-one days. The key thing was, I was going to Italy not only as Auditing Specialist, but also as an Italian interpreter!

The mission was to bring a military truck convoy to Italy over the Brenner Pass in the Alps. There was a lot of snow, so the trip was spectacular. When we arrived at the border I went in to the Italian border crossing office to present our official papers. I introduced myself to the two Italian soldiers in Italian … and right away they wanted to know if I was Sicilian. I explained that my parents were both from Trabia, Sicily. Well, these two soldiers were also Sicilian! They asked me to speak to them in Sicilian. They were so happy to be able to talk to an American who could speak their native language. We were given a great welcome to Italy!

In Verona, we were able to do some sightseeing. It is a beautiful city with side-walk cafes, a Coliseum, ancient walls and architecture, and the home of Romeo and Juliet!

After we completed our IG activities, we returned by car to Salzburg. When we arrived at the Brenner Pass checkpoint, the major called, "Rubino, come into the office." The Sicilian soldiers wanted to speak Sicilian with me again and wanted me to complete the papers for our return over the border.

The IG officers were thankful that I could speak Sicilian and had made the relationship at the border friendly, which permitted us smooth sailing. They reported to the Inspector General that I was very important to their successful mission, and the Inspector General called me into his office to congratulate me. I was so happy that I was able to act as an ambassador. God was certainly with me!

Brenner Pass checkpoint on the way into Italy.

Pete Armanini, Dante Marcolina, and me at Camp
Truscott in January 1954. The snow was really something!

I also got to travel extensively when I was *not* on duty—and there was one
place in particular that I really wanted to go. Remember, I had told my Mama
that I would visit our relatives in Sicily. So, in 1953 I took military leave and took
a train from Salzburg, Austria to Palermo, Sicily.

Since I was on leave I had to wear civilian clothes, so I had my parents send me
some of my favorite shirts, slacks, and coats. I traveled first class on the train, not
realizing I would be the only passenger in the compartment! It was beautifully
upholstered, though, and had a picture window. I had my camera and took pictures during the entire adventure. Beautiful mountains, villages, countryside, and
people made the ride great! The train had a dining car, too, which was a treat; I
ate to my heart's content.

What a fabulous experience. I traveled the entire length of Italy by train! Then,
when we arrived at the southern tip of Italy, we had to cross the Straits of Messina
by boat. But the boat had railroad tracks, so our train went with us—the railroad
cars were transported to the other side and onto the tracks in Messina, Sicily.

Once we were in Sicily, we traveled the north side of Sicily to Palermo, where
I planned to get off and rest up for the night. Just before Palermo, as the train
stopped at Termini Imerese (a station near Trabia), I opened the window and
took pictures of the local people on the train platform.

When I arrived in Palermo I took a horse-drawn carriage ride to a beautiful hotel that the driver recommended—the Grand Hotel et des Palmes. I can still hear the wheels on the cobblestone street. My room at the hotel was huge, with a large balcony, so I could take pictures of the street below. And apparently, this hotel was used as the headquarters of the famous mobster Lucky Luciano around this time, though I didn't learn this until many years later!

The next day I took a local train to Trabia, where I was hoping to spend a week meeting with both my parents' families—the Grecos, my Mama's family, and the Rubinos, my Papa's. When I got off the train there, I walked out of the station and asked the first person I saw for directions. She was carrying a large vase of water. I asked, "Do you know where the Greco families live?"

She put her vase of water down and hugged and kissed me! She was my Aunt Angela, married to my Mama's brother Ignazio. This truly felt like a religious moment, and the train station in Trabia has ever since been the "Enchanted Train Station" to me.

Angela notified the Rubino families of my arrival. I had not realized that Mama and Papa had already made arrangements for me to stay with Uncle Angelo Rubino and his wife, Rosa. Uncle Angelo told me that he thought I was going to get off at Termini Imerese, and that my father's brothers (Angelo, Antonino, and Mariano) were on the train platform in Termini Imerese the day before, looking for a soldier to get off. I told him I was not allowed to travel with my military uniform, and that I had gone on to Palermo to stay the night.

Well, you'll never believe it. Later, when I returned to Salzburg and had my pictures developed, I realized that the "local people" I had photographed at Termini Imerese on my first trip through were actually my uncles! I really felt something very magical had occurred.

During the week, I stayed with Uncle Angelo as planned. Aunt Rosa gave me their bedroom upstairs, which was very generous of them. I must explain that in 1953 the Rubinos and Grecos did not have running water or electricity. In fact, I remember that Uncle Pepe (Giuseppe) had a home with dirt floors, and the mule was stabled in a section of the one-room home! No one had running water, electricity, or a place to cook. Cooking was done outside on some stones.

I had to divide my time carefully between the two families. Apparently there was some sort of rivalry! On my first night, I was placed in the middle of Uncle Angelo's home, and the Rubino family gathered to hear about life in America. They said that they had heard "all you have to do is pick up gold off the streets." I told them that no, you had to work for money! I spoke for hours in Sicilian. Thank God I was fluent! Some friends who had been invited over thought I was born in Sicily since I spoke the classic Sicilian dialect.

At one point someone asked if I needed any water. I was talking so much that my mouth was dry, and I said yes. Well, I didn't realize that my cousin would have to go to the *town well* to get the water.

One day my Uncle Antonino Rubino and his family took me in a mule-drawn cart to the *campagna* (countryside) for a "pizza" outdoor picnic. It was wonderful—everything fresh and homemade. Another day my Uncle Angelo and his family took me hunting. I had my own shotgun and everything. We also had wonderful dinners together—the food was always so tasty and wholesome.

My Mama's family took me for a great walk to Termini Imerese to retrace Mama's footsteps. We stopped first at the beautiful church in Trabia where Mama would go with her mother. They had to pay a penny if they wanted to sit down. We also stopped to see a memorial to a saint where my Mama used to pray before going to Termini Imerese to visit relatives.

A "few" of the relatives on my Mama's side.

When we returned to Trabia, my Mama's family had a wonderful dinner complete with music. Mama's mother wanted to dance with me. She said that even though she had pain in her legs, she wanted me to be able to tell Mama that I had danced with her mother. As we danced I hugged her tight and she said to me, "*Chi tiene fede a Dio non perische mai*" (He who has faith in God shall never perish)!

I told her, "Mama taught me those same words."

She said, "I taught your Mama!"

It really impressed me that although they were poor, they were rich in faith!

One day my Papa's brothers took me to the spaghetti factory in Trabia, where we toured and saw the process of making spaghetti. It was something to see the long strands of spaghetti hanging to dry.

Another day my Mama's sister Angela climbed a ladder next to their house to pick grapes for me. Maria held the ladder for her. Another time they showed me the huge lemons that Mama used to tell me about in America.

Aunt Angela picking grapes, with Aunt Maria
(my Mama's sister) holding the ladder.

Both families took turns taking me to the wonderful memorial to Santa Rosalia (saint for the fishermen) right on the Mediterranean. Sea shells and stones were used to build it. At one point, as I was backing up to get a picture, I fell in the Mediterranean! I considered myself baptized.

The Santa Rosalia memorial on the Mediterranean.

Both families lived in the village and would go to the *campagna* to tend to their huge olive groves. The size of the olive trees was really remarkable: they are enormous, and branches extend out so far that they have to be supported with large sticks so that they won't break off. They say the trees date back to the days of Jesus Christ!

The olives were sold to make olive oil. When I was hunting with Uncle Angelo among the olive trees, I picked up a black olive and was surprised at how bitter it was, but at the same time I could taste olive oil. Later, he took me to the olive oil factory to see how they press the oil out of the olives.

Top: Sitting down to a picnic in the country with relatives on my Papa's side. From left to right: my cousin Ignacio, a friend, Uncle Antonino, my cousin Mariano, Uncle Angelo, my cousin Maria, my other cousin Maria, and Aunt Marianna. Bottom: Returning from the picnic by mule and cart.

I took so many pictures of my trip to Sicily. The greatest one I have titled *The Great Meeting, 1953*. I brought both grandmothers together, with me behind them with my hands on their shoulders. Mission accomplished! I felt like a peacemaker.

The Great Meeting, with (left to right) Papa's mother,
me, and Mama's mother.

After a wonderful week of memories for a lifetime, I left by train to go to Rome. When I arrived, I took a cab to the Hotel Mediterraneo. The cab driver recommended this hotel, and it turned out to be perfect. I learned that when traveling, it is important to stay in a hotel located near the sites you want to see, including restaurants and shopping. Time is so precious, and you want to be able to walk and take in the history.

I went to a travel agency to make arrangements for seeing Rome as well as Pompeii near Naples. I wanted to make sure I got to see Pope Pius XII, St. Peter's Church, and the Vatican.

Pope Pius XII was at his summer home in Castelgandolfo, so we went by bus. It was overcast and there was a good chance of rain. But rain or shine, I wanted to see the Pope!

As we approached the residence, I purchased rosary beads and medals for the Pope's special blessing. I wanted our family at home to share in this wonderful experience and blessing!

The Pope was so thoughtful. He came out earlier than he was scheduled to, to an overflowing crowd in the open courtyard. He spoke from his balcony in many languages and said he was praying to God to delay the rain, but that in case the communication to God was affected by the weather, he would speak to us now. He told us to think of all the people in our life who we would like blessed and to hold all our rosary beads and medals. He then had us kneel if we could, and gave us his special blessing. He said that if it rained, it would be Holy Water. I was hoping for some—and there were some Holy Rain Drops!

Pope Pius XII addressing the crowd from the balcony
at Castelgandolfo, 1953.

The next day I went to St. Peter's Church and the Vatican. I was overwhelmed by the size and sheer beauty of both! The church has a beautiful statue, *La Pieta,* done by Michelangelo and depicting the Blessed Mother with Jesus Christ after he was taken down from the Cross. The marble statue is exquisite, and you can see that over time Christ's foot has worn smooth, where tourist after tourist has touched it. The church has a beautiful altar, and through the altar there is a dove on a stained glass window. Imagine people from all over the world gathered to pay homage and pray for peace!

The Vatican was so inspiring. Michelangelo painted the ceiling of the Sistine Chapel while lying on his back. It is magnificent! While I was there, I noticed an artist painting something with a magnifying glass. She was looking at the ceiling and painting these wonderful miniatures, which she then encased in a brooch. I bought one for my Mama. She wore it very often, and when people asked where she got it she would proudly say I had brought it from Rome. I still have the business card of the artist. She wrote on it that her painting was the "Bleu Madonna."

Looking down the magnificent circular stairway in the Vatican.

This was my first trip to Rome, and I threw coins in the Trevi Fountain. I visited the Roman Coliseum and walked up and down and around this huge, remarkable structure. Our group toured the historic Roman Forum, and the Pantheon with the open ceiling. We spent a beautiful afternoon at Adrian's Villa with the majestic fountains.

They say that Rome was not built in a day. Well, you certainly cannot see it in a day! I spent four days on this trip and promised myself to *return* and *return*. There are so many things to see and so many opportunities to *feel* history.

One day we traveled by bus to Naples to go to Pompeii, the town buried in, and preserved by, deadly ash when Mount Vesuvius erupted in 79 A.D. Its excavations reveal a way of life preserved in stone.

As this was my first trip to Europe, I wanted to visit as many cities as possible. Florence, Italy, was high on my list—so much art, and so many sights to enjoy. The picturesque Ponte Vecchio ("old bridge") spans the Arno River. There are many shops on this bridge, especially gold jewelry stores. The cathedral and adjoining bell tower is spectacular.

The Medici family brought prosperity to Florence in the 1400s, and the city is a great example of the Renaissance. Names associated with Florence are Boccaccio, Dante, Galileo, Michelangelo, and Raphael. There are churches, palaces, museums, and so much more to keep you moving—a great education! As with Rome, you have to return to Florence to discover more of this wondrous city.

"Holding up" the Leaning Tower of Pisa.

Heading back north toward Leghorn (Livorno) is the city of Pisa. The Leaning Tower of Pisa is famous. It is the campanile next to the cathedral. The leaning tower "leaned" after it was built. I climbed to the top—293 steps!

I also visited Genoa, with its famous Porta Soprana and the home of Christopher Columbus. Genoa was bombed extensively during World War II and had to rebuild quite a bit, so it has many modern skyscrapers. It is a busy port and a mixture of medieval and modern.

Finally on my leave, I had always wanted to visit the beautiful and romantic city of Venice. I was definitely rewarded with a beauty that I will never forget. I have returned to Venice and I enjoy it more each time: the gondolas, canals, bridges, churches, the Grand Canal, and St. Mark's Square (Venice's only large square, paved with marble). On one side of the square is the Torre dell'Orologio with its clock. Two giant bronze Moors strike the hours with sledgehammers on a large bell. This has happened since 1497.

The ride along the Grand Canal with its historic buildings, mostly palaces and churches, is breathtaking. At night the restaurants around St. Mark's Square come alive with sidewalk cafes filled with happy customers, and some have musicians playing this wonderful music that you can hear from afar. Really romantic!

On St. Mark's Square is the famous, incredibly beautiful St. Mark's Church. When I entered the church I was so impressed with the "paintings," which turned out to be mosaics!

Gondolas off of St. Mark's Square in Venice.
What a beautiful city!

Later, in February 1954, I got to visit another part of Italy. Dante Marcolina, who also came to Austria as an Italian interpreter, invited me, Pete Armanini, and Lino Bruno (another Italian interpreter) to visit his relatives in Udine, Italy. Dante was born there and wanted us to share *his* reunion with his relatives. We took the train, and it was extremely cold. We were high in the mountains, which were covered with deep snow. We wore our heavy military-issue overcoats (commonly called "horse blankets") and we were still cold!

We took a taxi to the town of Maniago to visit Dante's relatives. Before leaving, we had roasted goat at our hotel restaurant. This was the first time I had had goat, and it was absolutely delicious.

When we arrived in Maniago, Dante's relatives treated us to a very strong drink to get us warm. The drink was grappa, and believe me, it was strong. We "warmed up" fast!

Dante was a very kind and considerate person, and so were his wonderful relatives, who made us feel right at home.

Fortunately, I was able to travel elsewhere in Europe as well. In December 1953, I took a trip to Garmisch, Germany. I visited the Olympic Ice Stadium, and even went ice-skating. What a thrill! I stayed at the Hotel Bahnhof, which had a balcony and a great view of the town below.

I visited the village of Oberammergau and went to the theater where the famous passion play is held. Also, I saw the Hansel and Gretel house, which has the story beautifully painted on it.

Another great highlight of my stay in Garmisch was a trip to the top of Germany's highest mountain—a two-mile ride via cable car, and not the kind that go along the ground like in San Francisco. Our little cable car was dangling in the air all the way up! The mountain is the Zugspitze, and it is about 10,000 feet high.

Before being allowed to take the cable trip, you have to enter a tunnel and show your passport and/or military leave papers inside the mountain checkpoint. On the way up along the cable, you have to exchange cabs midway—wow. What a transfer! There are steel structures built on the side of the mountain to support the steel cable that the car runs along.

At the top of the mountain there is a hotel, weather station, and power plant. Plus, there is a special cross that marks the top of the Zugspitze. From the top, you can see the tips of mountains located in Italy, Switzerland, Austria, and Germany. It is a moving religious experience! You feel you are close to Heaven. When you look down you may see small dots in the snow—these are people skiing at the bottom.

Another interesting journey I undertook in Germany was to go to the top of Eagle's Nest, Hitler's famous Tea House at 6,000 feet elevation.

I wanted to experience and see as much as humanly possible. In Berchtesgaden, Germany, I went for a salt mine ride in the caves. As we moved along in these small mine cars, we could put our hands on the side of the cave and taste the salt!

One day in June 1954, I was talking to Pete Armanini in Camp Truscott. Pete was just relaxing and I said, "Let's go to Paris!"

His eyes opened wide and he said, "I can't afford it!"

"Let's pool our money," I said.

I went to my room and brought back my "vacation savings" and put them on his bunk. I told Pete to put his vacation fund on the bed, which he did.

"I don't have as much as you," he said sadly.

But I combined the cash on the bunk and said, "This is *our* money to see as much of Europe as possible."

He was elated. "But how?" he asked.

To find out, we went to an Austrian tour agency in Salzburg and explained that we only had a few hundred dollars but we wanted to see as much of Europe as possible, starting with Paris, in about two weeks.

Our agent was wonderful. She explained that traveling second class by train would be our best bet for economy. She then booked us in a hotel in Paris in the section where artists, models, showgirls, and writers lived. We said, "Perfect!" Also, she arranged for us to rent a room in private residences in London, Brussels, Amsterdam, and Copenhagen. How great! We could meet the local people and see how they lived.

On June 18, 1954, we left Salzburg by train for Paris. What an adventure! Traveling second class allowed us to meet with travelers from all over the world and to see the wonderful landscape of Europe.

We arrived in Paris on June 19 and took a cab to our hotel, which was the type with a bathroom down the hall, not in the room. And now imagine this: our hotel was occupied by some of the dancers from the Moulin Rouge and the Folies Bergère! They were great in helping us to feel welcome in Paris. Obviously, we agreed to see them in their colorful and marvelous shows at the Moulin Rouge and the Folies Bergère. I still have the Moulin Rouge program, which includes the history of the Moulin Rouge: "The Bal du Moulin Rouge was inaugurated in April 1889, during the great Universal Exposition. It was in the Moulin Rouge that the famous dance French Cancan was born."

Because we had met some of the dancers at the hotel, it was special to see them do the Cancan. I love that music to this day, not only for its inherent excitement but for the wonderful memories.

We also promised to see some of the dancers at their Folies Bergère show—a tremendous production. We could only afford tickets for the balcony, so they advised us to rent binoculars. I'm glad we did!

The eye-catching program for the Moulin Rouge in 1954.

In Paris we also went on a nightclub tour, a city tour, and to Versailles. We went to the Eiffel Tower all the way to the top. It is only a few feet shorter than the Empire State Building in New York City. We also went to the top of the Arc de Triomph. We saw the show at the Nouvelle Eve Nightclub, and went to Pigalle.

Pete and I ate at sidewalk cafes and met people all the time from around the world. We met a Parisian who brought us to the Republique de Montmartre—famous for its cathedral and the many artists. He got us "Passports" to the district, and we went there by Metro (subway). We dined at La Brasserie Pigalle and drank with the local artists and beautiful models. It was fun trying to teach them English and learn French from them. We found out that if you smile and are friendly it breaks down any language barrier.

At the end of our fantastic stay in Paris, we set off for London on June 23, 1954. To cross the English Channel, the train boarded a ferry boat equipped with tracks—quite amazing. We were crossing at night, and as we approached the White Cliffs of Dover I got Pete out of his bunk to see them. We were determined to see as much as we could—to appreciate the moment!

In London we rented the living room of a private residence. It was well located, so we walked and walked. In fact, we walked all the way across London! We went to the docks and watched freighters being loaded and unloaded, and talked with some of the workers. We went to the Tower of London, Buckingham Palace, and Westminster Abbey. We took pictures of the guard at Buckingham. The guards are not allowed to talk or for that matter even smile. We boarded the famous double-decker buses, and we would always go to the top.

Piccadilly Circus was fun, with all the interesting people and the huge signs. We saw Big Ben, the famous clock. We went to dinner at a Spanish restaurant and nightclub and had our picture taken with an entertainer. We enjoyed the friendly nature of the people of London, and we could speak their language!

We arrived in beautiful Brussels, Belgium, on June 25, 1954, and checked into a room in a private home rented to us by a friendly retired couple. We did some sightseeing and we especially enjoyed the beautiful architecture. We went to the great Market Place and met people from all over.

On June 26, 1954, we arrived in Amsterdam, Holland. We checked into this marvelous home located on a canal. Our room was accessed via a spiral staircase! We spent three days at this great location. Each morning we were served a breakfast of cheese and a soft-boiled egg placed in a fancy container: the egg was upright and a hole was tapped into its top. We were treated royally!

We loved Amsterdam—the history, the architecture, the food, the canals, and the windmills. We went on a boat ride along the canal and had our picture taken for a memento of our stay.

Next we took a bus tour to the islands of Volendam and Marken. On the way, we saw these beautiful windmills. Near one in particular I saw a man fishing—a Kodak Moment! I asked the bus driver if he would slow down so that I could get the shot.

At first he said no. I couldn't believe it! But these wonderful ladies on board came to my rescue. They pleaded with the driver to stop, and he finally did. He allowed me to get off the bus to take the picture that I have titled *Windmill and Fisherman.*

I kneeled to take the picture between the bridge railings so that I could get clear shots. I had two cameras—one for color and one for black and white. One of the color prints was later awarded a prize in a photography show. And a famous photographer once saw it framed in my office and said that it was "museum quality" and that "it looks like a painting!" He wanted to know what camera I used; it was a Zeiss Ikonta bellows camera with a 3.5 Tessar lens, and I had to use a light meter—German make, Bertram Chrostar.

Windmill and Fisherman, black-and-white version, 1954.

This photographer belonged to the famous Bohemian Club in San Francisco. I told him that since I had to use a light meter to adjust for the lighting that day, I was taking longer than the bus driver wanted. In fact, he started driving away! Of course, my wonderful ladies made him stop.

The color print of *Windmill and Fisherman* has hung in my office, my home, and a photography show. I still have the slide, which is enclosed in a glass metal frame and was developed in Austria. I also still have the camera and light meter!

Marken and Volendam were interesting: the men actually wore wooden shoes. I bought souvenir miniature wooden shoes as gifts. We also saw the Peace Palace at The Hague in Holland where the International Court convenes.

Three residents of the island of
Marken in Holland. Notice the wooden shoes!

After our stay in Holland we proceeded to "Wonderful, Wonderful Copenhagen!" and found that this old song is truly accurate. We arrived on June 30, 1954, and saw the famous Little Mermaid sitting on a rock in the port area. We stayed at a private home in Copenhagen. Again, the hosts were kind, and interested to hear about the United States. We would sit in their living room and have great conversations. They told us to go to the Tivoli Gardens, and it was marvelous. We stayed until dark and enjoyed the festivities. On a bus tour we saw a stork nest on top of a house roof. We also saw historic buildings, statues, and the City Hall Square. A wonderful city indeed!

We returned to Salzburg on July 3, 1954—with a lifetime of memories, but with more to be made.

In September of 1954, I wanted to see more of Europe, so I went back to the Austrian travel agency to inquire about going to Spain. The agent showed me a flyer that read, "SPAIN BY BUS—14 days all-in only $135.00." The flyer also said, "SPAIN—the garden of Europe—should be covered by bus in order to really enjoy the charm of its romantic landscape and historical cities. This trip is rather strenuous, but it will linger in your memory for a lifetime!"

The flyer was absolutely accurate! This definitely was a highlight in my life. Can you imagine: a tour price of $135, from Zurich, Switzerland, back to Zurich, with included Bus-de-Luxe (a Swiss bus line) transportation, first-class hotels in Spain, good middle-class hotels in France, all meals, sightseeing, guide services, and all taxes. A single room was $4 extra (I elected this); room with bath all the way, extra $20. (Actually, most rooms did have baths and if they didn't, there was always one down the hall. I didn't have to pay the extra $20.)

One of the many amazing stops on the "Spain by Bus" tour.

I was the only American soldier on the bus. There were thirty-four people in all, including four young women from Switzerland! Gigi and the girls made the trip so enjoyable. We all got along as international friends—we talked and were interested in each other. Also, our guide was terrific! He spoke French, German, Italian, and English. I actually found his Italian better than his English, so I could use both languages to get his tour information.

Enjoying the "Spain by Bus" tour with Gigi (standing next to me),
Gigi's sister (with shawl), and others in our group.

The southern part of Spain was quite beautiful, particularly Seville, where I went to a bullfight. I wrote in a letter to my Mama, "They killed ten bulls (one at a time). It really is rather cruel and bloody to watch. I took pictures anyway." Near Seville the landscape is greener, with groves of olive trees, orange and lemon trees, grapes, and so on. It was an amazing trip, made even more amazing by the great company.

As much fun as I was having in Europe, I was happy to learn that I was scheduled to leave by train from Salzburg on October 20 to arrive in Livorno (Leghorn), Italy, by October 21. Then our boat would leave on October 23 for America!

Near the end of my tour of duty, a soldier in my unit at Camp Truscott by the name of Ken Venturi asked me to have dinner with him and his wife in their apartment in Salzburg. He was a great guy and I gladly accepted. His wife prepared a wonderful home-cooked meal!

Ken used to play golf with the generals since he was a skilled golfer. He was from Westlake in Daly City, California, and he asked if I would call his parents when I returned to the States, to let them know firsthand how he and his wife were doing. I told him I would be happy to. As it turned out, his parents invited me to dinner at Joe's of Westlake, which is a marvelous restaurant—great food, staff, and a very friendly atmosphere. I explained that Ken was playing golf with the generals and that he and his lovely wife were enjoying Salzburg.

Well, it also turns out that Ken Venturi, on his return to the United States, became a famous golfer and TV commentator! Plus, I later moved to Westlake, Daly City. (My brother was living in Westlake and as a real estate broker found me my home there.) So I would later take my Mama to Joe's of Westlake many, many times.

Our boat, the *U.S.N.S. General R. E. Callan,* left Livorno as scheduled on October 23, 1954. We stopped in Casablanca where we did some sightseeing. This time I took pictures of a snake charmer with a cobra!

Pete Armanini and Dante Marcolina were also on board, and it was great to have such good friends to make the voyage. During the trip—on October 31, 1954—we attended Roman Catholic services. It was an especially great moment to give thanks to God for all his goodness.

We had a fun time on board putting on a talent show, with the passengers being the "talent." I was asked to be Master of Ceremonies and to help with the organization of the show. I loved it! Especially when I introduced "Miss Trieste" to sing some songs. The boat was really rolling at that moment, and she asked me to hold on to her during her performance. Well, I gladly complied. The troops were howling! "Mr. Lucky!" they shouted. Miss Trieste sang beautifully and then thanked me. I replied, "You are welcome—it was my pleasure!" She was going to America to join her husband, whom she had met during his military duty in Europe.

Another great talent on board was Lemon of the famous Harlem Globetrotters. He did his magic with a basketball—rotating it with one finger. He was a hero to us!

Once we had arrived in New York, we did some sightseeing and then reported to Camp Kilmer. We received our orders to travel across the United States by train. Since I was a sergeant by this time, I was placed in charge of the group.

Wearing my sergeant stripes in Salzburg's beautiful
Mirabell Gardens, with Hohensalzburg Castle in the background.

We traveled by Pullman Sleeper, a train car with bunk beds. The first morning I brought the men to the diner. They all wanted eggs prepared sunny-side up. Well, the dining car steward wanted to give us a hard time, and said he would serve us scrambled eggs instead. I explained that we had had enough scrambled eggs in the mess hall, and we were looking forward to fresh eggs! He kept refusing, but I insisted, and when he realized that I was not going to give in, he finally gave us wonderful service and sunny-side up eggs. The men thanked me for standing my ground. I felt that we should be treated with respect!

All in all, it was an interesting trip across the United States—from New Jersey to California, traveling a northern route that included Chicago. I'm glad we went by train so that we could see our wonderful USA. We arrived in Ford Ord on November 9, 1954. At that point, we were released to civilian life—we went home and to our families! Thank you, God!

Grateful to be back home with my family, in front of our Banks Street flats.

Yet More Silver

In late November of 1954, after being released from the Army, I returned to the University of California in Berkeley to pursue my graduate studies. My plan was to earn a master's degree in Business Administration, specializing in accounting and marketing. Then I wanted to take the state CPA (Certified Public Accountant) exam and enroll in Boalt Hall Law School. I still wanted to be both a CPA and a lawyer, even though my plans had been interrupted by my service in the Army.

In life I find that change happens for the best. As I write my life story, I can see that I was being guided by God. I had an experience of a lifetime in my early twenties: I went to Europe, I met people from all over the world, and I had a great experience traveling and seeing my relatives in Sicily. And now, because of the GI Bill of benefits, my continued education would be paid for by the United States government—what a wonderful privilege!

I enrolled in and completed the graduate courses in Business Administration for the spring and fall semesters in 1955. I took advanced courses in Auditing, Accounting Theory, Labor Relations, Marketing, Organizational Theory, and Business Problems and Investigations. Also, I completed the final exam for the MBA and the Special Studies Report. This report was entitled "Mechanized Accounting and Its Effect on Auditing"—a topic that, in light of current national voting concerns, seems to apply today, some fifty years later! In the 2000 election, much attention was focused on the punched cards in Florida. In 2004 and going forward, there are still concerns with electronic, or "mechanized," voting—particularly, how to verify the results. Professor Moonitz, one of my accounting professors, at a meeting of the alumni a few years back, mentioned that perhaps I should prepare a Ph.D. thesis and a follow-up to my MBA report. Of course, today I would be able to draw on my experiences as Auditing Specialist for the Inspector General and on my experiences with Kaiser Steel, Kaiser Center, Kaiser Aluminum, and Cushman & Wakefield. Stay tuned!

I was awarded the MBA in June 1956—and soon after that came another major turning point in my life.

Practice 3

Write about a time when something didn't turn out the way you wanted it to. Consider what you gained from that situation that you may not have otherwise.

CHAPTER 4

JUST SAY YES! TO OPPORTUNITY

The year 1956 began with a decision that may sound crazy to some: instead of immediately continuing my education as I had planned, I shifted my focus by accepting a job in another city—without even knowing much about it! But as I look back, I see that my leap of faith here placed me on a path leading to one great opportunity after another.

Jump Right In

What happened was, the University of California held a Career Day Fair on campus in early January 1956—a few months before I was to be awarded my MBA. Major corporations had personnel there who were hiring for various job openings. I was interviewed by IBM, Pacific Telephone, Haskins & Sells, Kaiser Steel, and others. At this time, I was still planning to enroll in Boalt Law School and preparing to take the CPA exam. However, I was immediately offered positions with all of these corporations in their management training programs! So now I had a decision to make.

I recall going to offices for Kaiser Steel, Haskins & Sells, and Pacific Telephone. Haskins & Sells offered me a choice to go to New York or Los Angeles and the chance to pursue my CPA career. Kaiser Steel offered me a position as an Internal Auditor at a steel plant in Fontana, California, where I had never been in my life.

What to do? I thought about the fact that I was now twenty-five years old, that I had already experienced being on my own for two years traveling all over Europe, and that I had acquired great experience as Auditing Specialist for the Inspector General in Salzburg, Austria. And there was one more key factor: Kaiser Steel was one of the many corporations of Henry J. Kaiser, whom I admired greatly for his vision and for building the Victory Ships during World War II—ships that were instrumental in the war effort.

My decision: Kaiser Steel! And they wanted me to start right away, on February 6, 1956. It was exciting!

My Fort Ord buddy, Frank Terranova, offered to ride with me to Fontana, California. Imagine it: I took the job *sight unseen*. I grew up in urban, cosmopolitan, *foggy* San Francisco, and here we were in Southern California among orange groves and sunshine, with a steel plant right in the middle—Fontana! I had never been to a steel plant, and as we drove closer to Fontana we could see smoke stacks on the horizon. I checked in at the guesthouse, and in the morning reported for work! Just like that.

Although I was doing internal auditing, I was also part of the Management Training Program. I toured facilities and also received a plant orientation in Fontana. I wrote a report titled "Heating and Squeezing," summarizing what I had learned about the important role of heat and pressure in the processing of steel and other materials.

My activities weren't restricted to Fontana, however. Kaiser had many operations throughout California, so while I was assigned to the Fontana plant, I went on audits of the Eagle Mountain iron ore plant and the Montebello fabricating operation. At Eagle Mountain, we saw the open-pit excavation of the iron ore. I was amazed at the size of the equipment!

Soon after arriving in Fontana, I found an apartment in Pomona, California, on *Francisco* Street (what a coincidence). Its structure was similar to a motel, and it was owned and operated by a "Mama" and "Papa." My next-door neighbor was the grandmother who would prepare "extra soup" for me. She also introduced me to her granddaughter. They treated me like family!

I enjoyed my time in Fontana (though it surprisingly turned out to be short, as you'll soon see). I used to go for dinner to Vince's Spaghetti House in Pomona. The customers formed a line that went outdoors—it was that popular. It deserved its popularity, because the sauce was excellent. However, it was not as good as my Mama's!

Sometimes I would go to the Magic Lamp in Cucamonga. I loved their bread sticks coated with a cheese sauce and served hot. Marvelous! I also went bowling and met many of the steel workers. The restaurant at the bowling alley had great prime rib.

After only three months in Fontana, I was brought back to Oakland to replace an auditor who was being made Chief Accountant of the Napa Fabricating Plant. My "family" at the apartment was very sorry to see me leave. I thanked them for making my stay so comfortable. I gave them all a big hug!

Of course, Kaiser had told me in the beginning that I would probably spend a year in Fontana. So, I had gone to Sears and bought pots and pans, stainless steel flatware, Melmac dishes, bookcases, and a live plant! Oh well—I loaded everything in my Mercury and put the plant in the front seat, and set off back to the Bay Area.

First, though, I gave myself a holiday: I decided to visit Las Vegas on my way back to Oakland. I went across the desert, and whenever I found a gas station I would always put water in my plant.

Imagine: Las Vegas in 1956! I stopped at a diner on the strip, which was pretty undeveloped at the time. I sat at the counter for lunch, and the cowboy next to me started up a conversation. It turns out he was selling real estate and wanted to sell me some lots in the desert near the strip. And guess what: in this instance I *didn't* say yes to opportunity! I still kick myself today that I didn't take him up on his offer. Imagine owning land where all the major hotels are located in Vegas. In life, you never know when an opportunity will arise. Everything is timing!

When I left Las Vegas and headed back to San Francisco, I decided to drive across the desert at night so that it would be cooler. (My car did not have air-conditioning.) I was alone on the road, and I could see various animals cross in front of me—it was *pitch black*. It was just me and the headlights. I drove non-stop. Luckily there was a gas station on the way. "Fill 'er up and water my plant, please." This was when we had full service at the gas stations, even in the desert!

I reported to the Oakland office in May 1956. Herb Warren, the person who had hired me in Berkeley, was the General Auditor in charge. I learned that in addition to auditing the general books in Oakland, I would be responsible for the Napa Fabricating Plant and the coal mines in Sunnyside, Utah.

Visiting the coal mines in Utah was so interesting—really an adventure! My job there was to personally hand the payroll checks to the coal miners, to make sure there were "no dead men on the payroll" (in other words, to prevent fraud). So, I had to actually go down into the coal mines. It was eye-opening, and dangerous too. Prior to my going to Sunnyside, we had had some explosions "down under." I was alerted to listen to safety directions while down in the mines.

The Sunnyside homes were built for the miners, and the Manager of Mines invited me to his ranch. His home was a log cabin, and he had horses—it was like being in the old Wild West days!

Before leaving Utah, I was invited by Sunnyside management to dinner in Price, Utah, at a private club called Café Diamanti's Club. You had to ring a bell and were asked "Who sent you?" by someone looking through a peephole. Customers (members) brought their own liquor and left it at the club with their name on the bottle. Utah had strict liquor laws! We had the biggest steaks there—and tender, too.

I used to love to go to the Napa Fabricating Plant in the Napa Valley. Everybody there was like family—in fact, in general I was finding that working for Kaiser was like working for family. One of the superintendents in Napa took me under his wing and introduced me to everybody. I was made welcome, and my job was made easy because people there trusted me and were interested in my findings and recommendations.

We used to go to the Napa Airport for lunch and could see the airplanes take off and land. The restaurant is still there—some fifty years later. I especially remember the "Famous Jonesy" potatoes. They still have them. They put cheese on top of the potatoes on a hot grill, and a rock on top. Marvelous!

The superintendent was trying to get me to buy some land in Napa. Once again, I'm sorry that I couldn't say yes! In life, timing is everything.

Visiting the Mine Manager at his Sunnyside, Utah, ranch.

When I look back, I see that 1956 was really an important year in my life. When I returned to the Bay Area to work as an internal auditor for Kaiser Steel, I also went back to the University of California to enroll as a student in the Ph.D. program. At that time, the Graduate School in Business Administration was not offering a Ph.D. program. However, they recommended that I apply for the Ph.D. in Economics. I was accepted!

Dr. Kidner, my adviser, approved my working full time for Kaiser and agreed I could take a course each semester. He was wonderful! Kaiser was wonderful! If a course was taught only during the day, they would allow me to go to class. Also, our secretaries would type my term papers—they were wonderful!

However, my road to obtain a Doctorate in Philosophy did not exactly end on a wonderful note.

My transcript of my Doctor of Philosophy studies from 1956 to 1960 shows that I completed the required twenty-four units, though in different departments: twelve units in the Department of Economics, and twelve units in the Graduate School of Business.

Let me explain what happened. I was enjoying my stay in the Economics department. In fact, during the fall semester of 1957, I received an A grade from the Chairman of the Economics department, in the course "Fundamentals of Economic Theory" (Econ 200A), taught by Dr. Papandreou. (Dr. Papandreou, by the way, later became Prime Minister of Greece!) However, in 1958 I was approached by Professor Revzan of the Business School, who enlisted me to transfer to the Ph.D. in Business. I would be a "pioneer" in the program, since they had now decided to offer the Ph.D. for the first time. I discussed the situation with Dr. Kidner, and he approved the transfer since I could help the Ph.D. program in Business. This is why I completed twelve units in Business for a total of twenty-four units.

What happened next was a major disappointment. Dean Grether was my adviser and dean of the graduate school. He explained that since I had completed the required coursework, the next step was for me to resign my position with Kaiser and become a teaching assistant at the university! Working as a teaching assistant was a requirement that had never been mentioned to me, either while I was in Economics or as a condition of my transferring to Business. I was now told that if I couldn't do this, I would have to be on "Leave of Absence" from my studies.

I couldn't leave my position at Kaiser. The university was paying only about $150 a month for the teaching assistant job, and I was living at home and supporting my parents. My father was now in his seventies and not working. In those days, there wasn't any Medicare. Times were tough for my parents!

I told Dean Grether of the problem. He assured me I would be welcomed back when I could manage it. Now, I am retired and would consider a combination Economics-Business Ph.D. program. It is interesting, after coming back from Europe—serving in Austria and traveling to Spain, Italy, Sicily, Switzerland, France, Germany, England, Holland, Belgium, Japan, Taiwan, Mexico, Hong Kong, Thailand, Canada, Greece, Turkey, and so on—I developed an interest in international marketing and international peace. It would be something to pursue Ph.D. studies with a focus on "International Marketing—Road to International Peace." Stay tuned!

I want to stress my great disappointment at not being able to continue my job and complete the Ph.D. program. I felt that after all of my efforts and years of study, I was being deprived! I am prepared to sit down with University officials and discuss the possibilities now. I really feel that I can make a difference. Plus, students in the Ph.D. program today are allowed to hold down jobs.

At any rate, my memories of my Ph.D. studies are very fond ones. I enjoyed graduate school and my relationships with the other students and professors. In those days, the classes had very few students and were sometimes held at the professor's home, where we would be served tea. It was relaxing, and we could get to know each other and have open discussions.

One of the students, Ted Mah, was interested in pursuing his Ph.D. in finance. We had a class together that was taught in the evening. So, before class he and I would have dinner at a Chinese restaurant near campus. This restaurant, like many Chinese restaurants in the Bay Area, had one menu in English and a more extensive menu in Chinese. Ted would order from the *Chinese* menu. We'd have a banquet!

Another student I came to know was Franco Nicosia, who was working toward a Ph.D. in marketing—we enjoyed our conversations on many subjects.

One term, I contributed to a term paper on motivation titled "A Motivational Model of Human Behavior in Organizations." This was written at the home of Robert Fernn in Berkeley. We had a team of four to collaborate on this project. Bob's wife would always prepare coffee and cake for us. This was another reason I was so disappointed that I couldn't continue with the Ph.D. program: I enjoyed my interactions with students and professors, and plus I was able to bring *real business problems and challenges* from my Kaiser experiences!

I was always bringing examples of marketing brochures and other materials from Kaiser. One example is that Kaiser sponsored the very popular TV show *Maverick,* and I had literature promoting the show—I have always loved, always had a passion for *marketing.* Dean Grether recognized this in me, and when he learned I would pursue my career at Kaiser, he advised me to become Marketing Director. He said I was a natural, that I had a unique flair for marketing. I had received an A grade in Dean Grether's course, Business Administration 269A (Marketing Seminar—fall semester 1958). As my story unfolds, you will notice that I wanted to make Dean Grether proud of me. He definitely was a mentor to me. I always appreciated the fact that he said I would be *welcomed back* to the university when I could manage it. (Like I said, stay tuned!)

Make Work Fun

As I mentioned before, we definitely enjoyed a family atmosphere at Kaiser, and this made going to work a pleasure. While I was with Kaiser Steel, for example, we would have a housewarming party every time someone bought a home. Bob Walker, Controller for Kaiser Steel, encouraged this family atmosphere. And it was at one of these housewarmings that I met someone who would have a profound effect on my future! This was Frank Scarr, General Manager of the Kaiser Center development for the World Headquarters of the Kaiser Empire. Shortly after the party where I met him, Frank Scarr contacted me to offer me the job of Chief Accountant of the Kaiser Center project under construction!

What an opportunity to break into management of the Kaiser organization. Kaiser Center, which was completed in December of 1959, was to be the new headquarters for Henry J. Kaiser's various companies. It was a very big deal in the Kaiser organization: now we would all be located in one building! At the time, the building in the Kaiser Center complex (the Kaiser Building) was the largest office building west of Chicago, and it was built mainly out of Kaiser-produced materials (80 percent of the structure was made from Kaiser products like steel, aluminum, concrete, and gypsum). The complex would include a parking garage, an upscale cafeteria overlooking Lake Merritt, even a department store.

I accepted Frank Scarr's offer, of course! So from 1959 to 1966 I was Chief Accountant for Kaiser Center, Inc., and later promoted to Accounting Manager. I was directly involved with construction accounting during the actual construction phase of Kaiser Center, and then involved with the setup of the Chart of Accounts for operations. As Accounting Manager, I had full responsibility for the financial and operating statements for the entire Kaiser Center project.

I was very fortunate to work not only for Frank Scarr, General Manager, but also for Al Bava, Controller. They were both my mentors! When I started as Chief Accountant for Kaiser Center, we worked in a small building across from the construction site. Al and I had one construction accountant, Isabelle Zentner, who was terrific. We eventually moved to the Kaiser Building once it opened, and Al and I hired accountants, clerks, even *tour guides*. Yes, we actually gave public tours to people who came on Gray Lines buses.

Al and I used to work sometimes until midnight and then be back at 8:00 AM. Before the new building opened, we used to go into the steel structure and start planning for operational accounting. These were exciting times! We were like *family* as we opened the Kaiser Center. We were proud to be a part of Henry Kaiser's vision.

Here I am with the new
Kaiser Center in the background, in the 1960s.

The Kaiser Center was like a city: We had a medical clinic free to our employees. The cafeteria was operated by Mannings, and we subsidized the cost. We were allowed to go to the barber shop during business hours. (The story goes that Mr. Kaiser said, "Since your hair grows during business hours, you should be able to have it cut during business hours.")

We were family! I enjoyed going to work. Al Bava and I would go for walks at lunch and go to a small French café, Le Petit. In those days, you could get a filet of sole lunch for $1! The restaurant was located on Grand Avenue near the park on a tree-lined street. It reminded me of Europe. Al spoke fluent French, having been schooled and raised in France (though his parents were Italian).

Al Bava taught me practical applications of management. One morning he came to my office and noticed I was working on a spreadsheet accounting schedule myself—something one of my employees really should have been doing. He said, "John, you're the manager. I don't care if your desk is always clear—you should *manage*. Make sure the accountants are doing their job!" Lesson learned! I made sure that more than one accountant could do certain critical functions (for example, payroll and statistics), and I stressed that if you have free time, ask if you can help someone who is having a problem. What goes around comes around!

Nancy Perakis was a young accountant who was so anxious to learn more and would volunteer to learn the different functions in the accounting department.

With her great attitude, I knew she would be successful. She was intelligent and a quick learner—a key employee. The rest of my great accounting team included Sandy, Micki, Diane, Pat, April, Mort, Irma, Isabelle, Celina, and Johnnie.

It should be noted that Henry Kaiser believed in landscaping and open areas. In fact, he had told A. B. Ordway (Kaiser's first employee and Vice President of the Kaiser Center Project) that he wanted to look down on the top of the garage and see a beautiful landscaped garden. Hence, a 3.5-acre roof garden was included in the project. Mr. Kaiser wanted to give back to Oakland. Ordway took charge and made it happen!

We had gardeners on the payroll, and we set up our accounting controls to monitor those costs. We would allocate costs not only for gardeners but for electricity and water as well. Al Bava and I set up a Roof Garden Cost Control Center. We had a work-order system to accumulate costs of a particular job. We needed to be organized. You see, we had carpenters, operating engineers, painters, watchmen, laborers, tour guides/receptionists in the main lobby, carpet layers, garage personnel—in the early days we even had a gas station and mechanics. There was also a chauffeur's office for all the top executives of the various Kaiser companies. It was quite an operation!

Frank Scarr shared with me his experience of working with Henry J. Kaiser during construction. Frank would go to the Fairmont Hotel in San Francisco with samples of carpet and wall colors, and Mr. Kaiser would personally pick out his choices! Later, after we moved into the new building, Frank Scarr introduced me to Mr. Kaiser in the executive dining room. I remember that Mr. Kaiser said, "Keep up the good work as Chief Accountant—we need you."

We began moving into the new Kaiser Building on December 21, 1959. That year, I was one of the directors of the Kaiser Employees Club, and Ann Trtan and I were co-chairmen for the 1959 Christmas Dinner-Dance. What an exciting time! The *Home Office* publication (put out by Kaiser Services Public Relations) reported:

> More than 700 Kaiser people and their friends took over the Garden Court of San Francisco's Sheraton-Palace Hotel December 18 for the Kaiser Employees Club 1959 Christmas Dinner-Dance.
>
> Co-chairmen John Rubino and Ann Trtan termed the affair "an elegant dance with couples remaining on the floor right up until music ended at 1 AM."
>
> A Latin combo spelled off the Glenn Miller orchestra, providing continuous rhythms for the dancers. Two rooms on either side of the Garden Court were opened up for dining.

The next year, the 1960 dinner-dance was held December 10, again in the famous Garden Court of the Sheraton-Palace Hotel. Del Courtney's sixteen-piece orchestra set a dancing beat until 1 AM. Ann and I were also involved in this beautiful event. We had to meet with hotel staff to work out the arrangements for the dinner and orchestra. I remember that the Garden Court required that we hire the orchestra through the musician's union! Great experience. Again, a family atmosphere prevailed!

What a pleasure it was to go to work—something new every day! When we first moved into the Kaiser Building in 1959 and 1960 (different departments moved on different dates), the employees were inspired to dress up. It was a "fashion show" every day! Morale was high. Whereas before we were operating in twenty-six different buildings, now we were in one beautiful Kaiser Building. In addition to phone calls, we could see each other in person.

We also enjoyed activities like art shows, and even variety shows. The Employees Club sponsored art classes by Warren Brandon, and I enrolled along with Sylvia and Marita of Kaiser Center. At the time (1963), we had vacant floors with concrete flooring—ideal for art classes, since we couldn't harm the floors with our oil painting spills.

I created a number of oil paintings in these classes and signed them "Yano." (My parents and relatives often called me *Yano*, which is a short version of my Sicilian name, Mar*iano*.) Warren Brandon was inspirational—he used to show off my paintings. He said I had a unique, distinctive "Yano style." He advised me not to take lessons because it would take away from my style. He encouraged me to paint my way! I did enter my paintings in art shows and I did receive ribbons. I was even offered money for one of my paintings, but I didn't want to sell. I highly recommend painting—it is so relaxing, creative, and rewarding.

Speaking of art and creativity, let me share a story about a woman who used to work for me: Faye Potter. Faye became a successful painter later on, and I cherish the fact that when she was interviewed about her art by the Kaiser Sand & Gravel *Conveyor* publication, she gave me credit for encouraging her.

Here's what happened: Faye worked for me in the accounting department, and one day I noticed she was sketching at her desk. I had a glass wall in my office, so I could see what she was doing, and I called her on my phone and said, "Faye, please come into my office and bring what you are working on."

She was so nervous! She was worried I was going to reprimand her. But actually I wanted to talk to her about her sketches, which were great. I asked if she painted, and she said no. I told her she had real, natural talent and that she should try it. She did, and became very successful—selling her paintings! She gave me a painting as a thank you, and I treasure it. I'm so proud of her!

Truly another morale booster at Kaiser were the variety shows we put on in the Oakland Auditorium. I was involved not only with organizing them but also as an actor—what great fun! We had everybody involved: management, secretaries, accountants, and so on. We rehearsed on a vacant floor. I still have programs and pictures, which depict not only the actual shows, but also the great cast parties! You see, this activity gave us something to talk about for years. I still cherish the memories to this day.

In one show, called *It's a Date,* I played "Mr. I. Gott Rocks, President of the Alumni at Boola Boola." My character was supposed to wear a raccoon coat, and at rehearsal I was wearing a rental coat that was literally shedding. Henry Kaiser's secretary, Edna Knuth, came to my rescue—she somehow acquired a beautiful raccoon coat for me to wear. She said that she couldn't tell me who it belonged to, but considering whose secretary she was, I could probably guess! Edna played Hedda Hopper, Commentator, in the show.

Performing in *It's a Date,* along with other Kaiser employees.
Notice the raccoon coat!

In addition to *It's a Date,* we had other variety shows:

- *Shooting Stars,* April 8–9, 1960, in which I played "Steve Allen, Director, Nationwide Television, Inc."

- *Running Wild,* October 4–5, 1962, in which I played "Matt Lewis, the doctor, Chairman of People's Party impersonating the French Maid." Bert Morgan played Chuck Chamberlain, the disc jockey who masquerades as the Lady Mayor.

I was especially privileged to be the Master of Ceremonies at a show for servicemen and their families at Hunters Point in San Francisco. We had a variety of talent that was a success. This was done through the Kaiser Employees Club as part of our community outreach program. I started with "This is what they call a 'command performance'! Hello, Navy!" I introduced the acts and I even had a *comedy routine.*

We had a wonderful time producing all these shows. It brought us together as a team!

Practice 4

If you have a career already, what are some small things your company could do to inject some fun into the atmosphere and boost morale? Make a list of ideas.

Now make another list of activities that already exist—such as a company sports team—and consider how joining might affect your outlook.

CHAPTER 5

FIND A WAY TO DO WHAT YOU LOVE

I'm so glad I always took the opportunity to join in on activities like the variety shows and housewarming parties. I can see that because I was always willing to participate, to interact with people, and to try new things, I eventually was able to make marketing—a passion of mine!—a focus of my career. Here's how it happened.

Real Estate Yields Real Opportunities

In 1966, Frank Scarr, the Vice President and General Manager for Kaiser Center—whom I had met at that housewarming party several years before—asked me to become his assistant and learn the real estate business! He wanted me to be the spokesman for Kaiser Center. My official business card read "Assistant to the Vice President and General Manager."

Frank wanted me to start by observing his leasing and negotiating style. I did, and then officially began to assist in all property management matters related to the Kaiser Center and to another Kaiser-owned property, the 1924 Broadway Building. My new duties included not only leasing the office space in these buildings, but also handling tenant and public relations. (I had been active in the Building Owners and Managers Association, or BOMA, since 1964, and I had proven myself to be knowledgeable about various building management issues, at least from an accounting standpoint.)

The 1924 Broadway Building in particular was a wonderful experience because I was in charge and responsible for management. This had been a key building for the Kaiser group of companies. Henry Kaiser had made it his head-quarters while in Oakland until 1960, when, as you may recall, all the Kaiser administrative home-office functions were moved to the new Kaiser Center. The only Kaiser entity still remaining in the 1924 Broadway Building were the Kaiser Hospital offices.

International lawyer Joe Yovino-Young had set up his offices in Henry Kaiser's former offices in the Broadway Building penthouse. On one wall, Joe had a beautiful mural depicting his gorgeous Rome office, which even had a balcony, and his desk top was of *Carrara marble*. Joe was Sicilian and he used to like to talk to me in Sicilian. He would say, "John, you speak the *classic* Sicilian dialect." When I returned to Europe for a month-long adventure in 1970, he gave me a great list of his favorite restaurants in *Roma*!

I began my new position in leasing at an exciting time: the plans for the Kaiser Mall had been announced in August 1965, after the White House department store went out of business in San Francisco and the branch in Kaiser Center had to be closed. At that time, Frank Scarr—soon to be my boss—was quoted in an internal publication as saying, "We are converting the department store building into an attractive, self-contained complex of more than fifteen quality retail and specialty shops, commercial offices, and a restaurant." The same article notes that Arnold Michaels, president of Grodins department store, was so impressed with the Kaiser plans that he dropped his intention to move to a Broadway location and switched to Kaiser Mall, stating, "It is one of the most exciting projects we've seen."

Work started on the Kaiser Mall in October of 1965. The biggest task was the extensive alterations to the air-conditioning and electrical systems.

Key tenants in addition to Grodins were Expectations Maternity Shop, Merle Norman, Bay Ticket Office, Hallmark Cards, Dorothy's, and Janko Jewelers. The new restaurant, the Mirabeau, went into the third floor overlooking the Roof Garden, and was a true fine-dining establishment. The Kaiser Mall connected directly with the parking garage and with Joseph Magnin, another department store. With a total area of 22,600 square feet on the main and mezzanine floors, Grodins was surpassed in size only by the Joseph Magnin, which had 29,400 square feet.

There were two memorable persons that I was privileged to meet with regards to the Mall. Debbie Fields, the famous cookie operator, came to see me with her husband regarding a shop space for her new venture. I was so impressed with her enthusiasm! I brought them to lunch at our beautiful new Mirabeau Restaurant overlooking the Roof Garden. She asked if I thought she could be successful located in the Kaiser Mall. I told her that as much as I would love to lease the space to her, in all honesty, I felt that we didn't have the foot traffic she would need. I felt she could do better in a large shopping center that is open seven days a week and longer hours. She thanked me for my advice. Later on, it really proved to be the right advice—she became extremely successful!

Another memorable individual is Dr. Stewart Ritchie. Dr. Ritchie graduated from Stanford Medical School as a surgeon. However, he used to make sandwiches to support himself through medical school, and he developed a great reputation for his sandwiches. So, Dr. Ritchie capitalized on this and started the Guckenheimer Restaurant chain. He leased retail space in our Mall and also in the 1924 Broadway Building. He was very successful—a wonderful person! We used to say, "As a surgeon, he could really cut thin roast beef!" He enjoyed the humor. He always had a warm, caring personality.

Gail Holland was another great person I met in connection with leasing out Mall space. She organized Golden Gate Apple School in 1977, and I met her because she considered leasing space at Kaiser Mall for this project. Well, the Kaiser Mall rates were really too high for her budget, but we had lunch a couple of times and I gave her advice on the rental market.

Later, when she heard I would be attending a BOMA convention in New York, she arranged for me to go to a New York Yankees game and meet the owner, George Steinbrenner! You see, Gail's stepfather, Mr. Rosen, worked for Steinbrenner. So I got to sit in a box seat, and Mr. Rosen brought me to Steinbrenner's office, where we had a great meeting. Thank you, Gail, for a truly memorable event!

In the early years of my leasing and building management experiences, I attended the International Parking Association convention in Las Vegas. It was literally a 24-hour experience! Bill Logan of Kaiser Center also went, and he and I attended Midnight Mass, stayed up until all hours, and then attended the first seminar that same morning. God gave me the energy!

The late 1960s brought a lot of changes for the Kaiser organization—somber ones and promising ones. In 1967, Mr. Henry J. Kaiser passed away at age eighty-five, though his son Edgar continued to take charge of the company as he had for some time. The next year, a new building—soon to be called the Ordway Building—was announced, and scheduled for completion in September 1970. This change in particular proved to be a great opportunity for me, because the company needed someone to manage and lease out the space! So in April 1970 I was promoted to Leasing Manager and became responsible for this exciting new structure.

The Ordway Building was named after Henry J. Kaiser's first employee, A. B. Ordway. Upon its completion, Kaiser Center would include two high-rise structures plus the Mall.

I remember being invited by A. B. Ordway to his offices to have coffee and discuss the leasing and tenant relations of Kaiser Center. He was personally *involved* and was personally *supportive*.

Marvin Starr and Harry Miller were pioneer tenants in the Ordway Building. We were proud to tell other prospective tenants that they had signed our lease without any changes. They said, "We think it's a *fair lease*"!

Yanello & Stanwyck, attorneys, decided to become tenants and wrote a letter that made us proud that we were doing the right thing. We were on track!

My assistant, JoAnne Kearns; A. B. Ordway; and me posing with a model of the Ordway Building, which would be completed in 1970.

I was very proud of some of our Ordway law practice tenants. Many of them—Betty Deal, Donald McCullum, and Bill Dunbar—would later be appointed as judges! I was invited to their swearing-in ceremonies and received special thanks for my tenant relations.

Joe Morgan, a baseball hero, was another of our tenants and did wonderful work with youth activities.

Al Davis and Al Lo Casale of the Oakland Raiders football team were my guests for a personal tour of the Ordway vacant offices. We were trying to get Al Davis to become one of our tenants. He eventually found space closer to the Coliseum, but thanked me for a "great tour."

The FBI was also one of our original tenants in the Ordway. When Charlie Parker, the agent in charge of the Oakland office, was promoted to a position in Washington, D.C., I received an invitation to his party at the Presidio in San Francisco. At the party, he thanked me from the podium for all of my assistance.

As you can see, I have wonderful memories of my leasing activities. A lease is a legal document, but more important is the relationship with the tenants!

In Real Estate, It's Location, Location … Promotion

In 1978, a man named Tim Preece became President of Kaiser Center, Inc., and he would *definitely* become one of my mentors. I must give credit where credit is due!

When Tim Preece took over, he interviewed me and asked me to describe my duties. He was quick to realize that my title of Leasing Manager did not adequately describe the scope of my activities. For instance, during my time at Kaiser, I was always very involved with community outreach in Oakland and belonged to numerous organizations. He pointed out how important this was—working to make Oakland more attractive as a place to live and do business—and he came up with a new title for me: Manager of Leasing, Marketing, and Promotion. And the next thing he said was that I deserved a big raise!

In our meeting, we also discussed promotional tactics, and he asked me to publish a magazine around Kaiser Center. He gave me full responsibility to be creative. Wow!

I had a great assistant, JoAnne Kearns, and the two of us started to plan. We worked together as a team. First, of course, we needed a writer, but he or she had to be more of a reporter! We put out "feelers" and interviewed several candidates—and I honestly feel that God guided Colin Davies to our office. When he arrived and sat in the chair in front of us, I couldn't help but notice that his shoes didn't have *soles*. So I asked him what happened. Colin explained that he drove a Vespa scooter and the brakes didn't work, so he would stop by putting both feet on the ground—a logical explanation of worn soles!

JoAnne and I liked him right away. There was a chemistry—we could talk, and he was honest. Tim Preece approved him also, so we began to work on our magazine. What an adventure! We came up with the name *Kaiser Center Newsbreak* (instead of a coffee break, let's have a newsbreak!). And I had always enjoyed *Life* magazine with its distinctive cover picture. So, we agreed to always have a full picture as the cover.

Colin was a great photographer and a great reporter. JoAnne and I would meet with him in our office and then we would have lunch at the Mirabeau Restaurant overlooking our Roof Garden. The luncheons were a great morale booster and proved to be creative! Over the years, our *Newsbreak* issues would chronicle the happenings at Kaiser Center and all of the wonderful community outreach and public relations activities Kaiser sponsored.

Newsbreak was our "outreach" publication! I served as Editor, JoAnne was Assistant Editor, Colin was Publication Coordinator, and Tim Preece was the

Publisher. We promoted not only the shops and Kaiser Center, but also Oakland. We had a mailing list of San Francisco Bay Area tenants, politicians, and so on. All of our tenants received a copy. All of our employees received a copy. We had great communication! Whenever possible, the janitors at night would put a *Newsbreak* on the desk of every employee and tenant. In "confidential offices" we would leave the issues with the receptionist.

Eric Hubert of St. Paul Towers' top management supported us at the Mirabeau, often arranging birthday parties and other events there for the residents of St. Paul Towers, an apartment complex for seniors that was located near Kaiser Center. We provided him with copies of *Newsbreak* for the Towers' residents. We enjoyed his company at the Mirabeau and appreciated his opinions—he was a very good friend!

The Kaiser Center sponsored or played host to numerous events and activities—many of which I was involved with—so we always had something to report on in our *Newsbreak* issues. For instance, Christmas was always a very big time of year. We would have professional ice-skaters perform on an ice rink on the Roof Garden. We had special ice-making equipment installed, and the shows would bring crowds. The children loved it! The White House department store and Joseph Magnin store shared the cost with us. This was great for public relations and great for business!

During Christmas one year, we controlled the appearance of the front of the Kaiser Building by drawing some draperies and leaving others open at night, spelling out the word "NOEL" with the open, lighted windows. This was a beautiful sight, and we used this image as our *Newsbreak* cover photo—then inside the issue we included pictures of our nativity scene and of Santa up at the Kaiser Building rooftop.

Burton Weber, Special Events Coordinator for the Oakland Office of Parks and Recreation, was instrumental in supporting JoAnne and me in the Christmas shows in our Kaiser Center Auditorium. The whole community was invited to this annual event. And guess who got to play Santa Claus! I performed as Santa for this event each year from 1979 to 1983.

This was really a total entertainment package, and the photos we published in *Newsbreak* gave a good idea of the joy the children got from the experience. I myself was one happy fella to play Santa Claus. I used to pick up the Santa Claus candy (chocolate covered with foil featuring a picture of Santa Claus) and give those out. Some parents would tell me in advance their children's names and what their children wanted for Christmas. What a great surprise when I would tell the children, "I know what you want, and I know that your name is Johnny," or Mary, or whatever it happened to be. They loved it!

Then there was the memorable child who handed me a list and said, "You didn't bring me what I wanted last Christmas—so here's my list so you won't forget!"

In 1981 I began playing Santa Claus for an even bigger event. That was the year we launched "Christmas in Oakland": grand, citywide holiday events including a parade, tree lightings, and more. This was sponsored by the Chamber of Commerce as well as other businesses and community members, not just Kaiser.

Cornell Maier, a Kaiser executive, was *extremely* supportive and instrumental to the success of "Christmas in Oakland." I was co-chair of the event with the famous Irene Sargent (a well-known Oakland personality at that time, known as a fashion maven and for her civic involvement), and the two of us met with Cornell Maier to discuss the events. He asked if we needed financial support—the answer was yes! He came through with flying colors—and money! He was our *hero*.

Riding with Irene Sargent in a beautiful vintage car for the "Christmas in Oakland" parade.

Also, credit must be given to community leader and great supporter, Blair Egli, the Senior Vice President and Manager of Bank of America's Regional Commercial Banking Center, in the Oakland Main Office. Blair arranged for Irene and me to talk to key Oakland bankers to enlist their assistance. Blair held the meeting in his boardroom. I greeted everyone with "Merry Christmas!" Then we made our presentation of the series of events, and displayed pictures of the decorations we wanted to include. This was a fruitful meeting: Irene and I got their wonderful support!

Back at Kaiser Center, we would coordinate events and activities that were of interest to the public throughout the year, not just Christmas. For instance, JoAnne Kearns and I used to coordinate art shows at Kaiser Center. We had shows in the Kaiser Building, the Kaiser Mall, and in the lobby of the Ordway Building. The Ordway lobby was perfect for sculpture, and so was the Roof Garden.

At one point, we wanted to host a sculpture exhibit by the artist Bufano on the Roof Garden. This presented some interesting challenges! We had to figure out how to support the heavy weight of his sculptures, how to bring them up to the Roof Garden, and how to provide adequate security and insurance. We met with Bufano at Jack's Restaurant, where I was seated next to him. We had a great conversation about his career, and he was interested in my Sicilian family upbringing. We enjoyed each other's company! He rewarded me with an autographed copy of his book, *Bufano*, which has some marvelous pictures of his work.

Unfortunately, due to the many challenges, we were unable to bring the exhibit to Kaiser Center. But I was privileged to have met such a great artist.

Another favorite memory I have of our public relations activities was when Don Sherwood, a famous local radio disc jockey, called me about setting up his "mobile studio" at Kaiser Center. This would be great public relations, so JoAnne Kearns and I made the arrangements, including space, power, and publicity.

After the show, we invited Don and his staff to have breakfast at Manning's Cafeteria on the second floor of the Kaiser Building overlooking Lake Merritt. Don was so concerned about his casual attire. He pointed out that he had a hole in his sweater! I assured him that it would *not* be a problem—he was my guest! Months later, I received a personal invitation from Don to KSFO's employee Christmas party at the "Top of the Mark" in the Mark Hopkins Hotel, atop Nob Hill in San Francisco. Gene Autry owned the radio station and the Mark Hopkins Hotel, and he was at the party!

Don introduced me to Gene Autry and explained that I had helped him to put on a successful show at Kaiser Center. Gene Autry thanked me and asked for my business card. A few days later, Gene Autry sent me his famous Christmas record with his famous songs! I still have that record, and I play it every Christmas. Wonderful memories—wonderful people!

The different companies within the Kaiser group sponsored or put on their own public relations events and activities, so there really was always something going on to report about in *Newsbreak*. One year I became involved in a series of events related to Kaiser Aluminum's sponsorship of "Western Night" with the Oakland A's baseball team. The main event was of course the baseball game itself, scheduled for the evening of Friday, June 26, 1980. However, a couple of weeks before the game, we had a pre-celebration during the workday called "Western Rally Time." This was held around lunchtime and people were invited to bring their lunch to the Roof Garden for the entertainment: we had Western swing dancing and square dancing and music, and I was the Master of Ceremonies, dressed as the Rhinestone Cowboy!

For the game itself, Western Scenic provided professional Hollywood backdrops to create an old-town atmosphere of the Wild West. In this colorful atmosphere at the Oakland Coliseum, we provided square dancing, food, and music.

Again as the Rhinestone Cowboy, I went to the pitcher's mound on the field and performed as Master of Ceremonies. My job was to dispense $10,000 in gift drawings that were being given by Kaiser Aluminum. I awarded the "gifts" by calling out ticket numbers.

I remember when Cornell Maier, Tim Preece, Kaiser Aluminum attorneys, and myself had a meeting regarding giving away these gifts at the game. It was at that meeting that the attorneys advised us that, for legal reasons, we should not call the giveaways "prizes" but refer to them as "gifts." It just goes to show you: you have to consider so many facets when planning an event!

Dressed as the Rhinestone Cowboy for Western Night with the Oakland A's.

With all the events in which I was involved in Oakland, I know that success comes down to the cooperation of people dedicated to making an event happen. Carl Finley, Executive Vice President of the Oakland A's (cousin of the owner of the A's, Charlie Finley), had worked closely with me—he was great! And Jorge Costa was so helpful in accommodating us at the Coliseum. Billy Martin was a wonderful, colorful coach. He was generous with his time and signed a poster with his picture—I treasure it!

Tim Preece suggested we hire the locally famous "Crazy George" to be a yell leader at the game. So, JoAnne Kearns and I contacted George and made the arrangements for his appearance. He was amazing! The total event was terrific. We succeeded in increasing the attendance to the game.

JoAnne and I also hosted luncheons at the Mirabeau Restaurant with the Oakland A's players' wives, to plan a night at Children's Fairyland for the Oakland A's children. A's wives Terrie Langford, Brenda Murphy, Diane Newman, and Debbie Picciolo; Kaiser Aluminum management wives Claire Knipe, Mary Helen Smith, and Maedine Turner; and a few Kaiser Aluminum staff members were actively working with us. The event turned out well, and I received a wonderful thank you note from the A's wives.

Everybody won with these events—it was all so worthwhile!

The year after I performed as the Rhinestone Cowboy, Tim Preece asked me to arrange an official float entry by Kaiser Center for Oakland's St. Patrick's Day Unity Parade. Tim gave me and JoAnne Kearns full responsibility for the float, from picking a theme to building the float to assembling a team to ride on it.

We arranged for a great professional, Clarence Palmer of Palmer Displays, to work with us. But we still needed to pick a theme. We brainstormed and I remembered that wonderful Disneyland song, "It's a Small World." We decided on: Kaiser Center, "It's a Small World"—*Diverse and Unified*. We capitalized on the fact that this was a Unity Parade. We had Clarence construct large models of the Kaiser Building and the Ordway Building and place them on a large flatbed trailer to be towed by truck. Meanwhile, we assembled our team of people to ride on it.

On the day of the parade, March 14, 1981, we played a music tape of "It's a Small World" over loud speakers as we rolled along. And we had asked our team of "diverse" employees to dress up in colorful costumes! Being Italian (Sicilian), I of course became Christopher Columbus. JoAnne was a Spanish dancer, and Tim Preece was the Music Man. All of our Kaiser employees and their children were dressed in costumes and were truly great! And we weren't the only ones who thought so: Kaiser Center's entry won *first place* as the best commercial float and also won the parade chairman's special trophy!

Top: Dressed as Christopher Columbus to ride on our St. Patrick's Day float. Bottom: Our amazing float, with models of the Kaiser Building and the Ordway Building.

I truly enjoyed promoting Oakland, and I was always looking for ways to increase the value of this city as a location for business. So I was pleased to be involved with a very exciting project: Kaiser Airline Center, largest in the nation!

This was a historic happening, both for Kaiser Center and for Oakland. Imagine having eleven major airline ticket offices working side by side. This had long been a dream of mine, and with the help of many people, it became a reality on April 23, 1982!

Tim Preece, our President, and Bonnie Guiton, who had recently been named Vice President and General Manager, supported me all the way. JoAnne Kearns, Brent Harker (Kaiser Center's Superintendent of Space Planning), and I worked with all the airlines, which enthusiastically endorsed the concept. In fact, we never had to solicit a single airline—once word got out, they called *us* wanting to become involved.

However, putting it all together was not easy. In fact, a project like this would be worthy of a Donald Trump *Apprentice* assignment! Not only did we have to move some of our current tenants to other spaces to open up a big enough area for the Airline Center, but we also had to orchestrate all the details with eleven independent airlines, from the planning, leasing, marketing, and construction to the celebration of the opening!

What a great ceremony for the grand opening—all the airlines participated and contributed entertainment and gifts. This was a huge event! We had a Dixieland band, hula dancers, a mariachi band, traditional Japanese dancers, and more. During the planning of it, JoAnne and I held regular meetings with marketing representatives and even the police department. You see, certain streets had to be closed off for the main event: a noontime fly-over of World War II–era planes!

After the Kaiser Airline Center opened and the ceremonies were a great success, I received an invitation from Tom De Caro, Marketing Director for American Airlines, to be a guest on their inaugural flight to Honolulu. Tom was so pleased with our organization of the event, with total participation of the airlines and community leaders.

Before our departure from the San Francisco Airport, the airline had arranged various festivities, and I had a photo taken for posterity. Dwight Clark of the San Francisco 49ers football team, famous for his winning catch of a pass from Joe Montana in the 1982 NFC Championship Game, was also there.

When I got back from Hawaii, I wrote a thank you letter to Tom De Caro for the *marvelous* experience! I was in the first-class section, complete with swivel chairs, hula dancers, and live music, all the way to Honolulu. Chateaubriand roast beef with all the trimmings was served. In my letter to Tom, I explained that I had had to return to San Francisco for a high school reunion—on the very next day! I wrote, "During my whole lifetime, I'll be able to recount the time I flew to Honolulu for dinner and returned the next day—a real jet-setter."

It's interesting that while I started out in accounting, I ended up in real estate, and found that marketing, which I am naturally drawn to, plays a key role in that field. Remember, I had enjoyed studying marketing while working toward my Ph.D. at Berkeley, and now here I was using my skills every day!

Franco Nicosia, whom I had met while we were both enrolled in the Ph.D. program at UC Berkeley, later became a Professor of Marketing there himself. So, during the fall quarter of 1981, he invited me to address his marketing class for the *full hour*. Afterwards he sent me a thank you letter, stating, "I want to stress that you put across not only the professional aspect of your work but also those human qualities that have become so rare these days: enthusiasm, involvement through hard work, and honest idealism." What a thoughtful letter!

My topic that day was "Oakland: a City for Sale." I addressed the need for a public relations program for selling the positive aspects of Oakland. It was truly a great opportunity for me, not only to share my message of promoting Oakland, but also to revisit my old alma mater and address the students as a marketing expert!

Practice 5

Make a list of some activities that you truly enjoy doing—for example, writing, interacting with people, playing video games, photography, solving mysteries, cooking.

Now take a close look at each item in your list. Brainstorm some ideas for using your skills in these areas at your current job (you never know where it could lead!), or brainstorm some other real jobs that have these activities as an element. If you need some extra help, consider talking to a career counselor, who can probably tell you about opportunities you never even realized existed.

CHAPTER 6

DO DINE OUT

Looking back, I notice that with dating, building business relationships, and celebrating friendships, I've always involved dining out and sharing good meals. I would always take clients to our Mirabeau Restaurant at Kaiser Center, and I enjoyed sharing lunches with my co-workers. Conversations are easier over a meal and, particularly important if you're on a date, you can really get to know each other! Good food is so important—and so important to share.

Dating and Dining

Many of you may remember Herb Caen, the famous columnist for the *San Francisco Chronicle* from the 1930s to the 1990s. Herb Caen was an expert on San Francisco, and I read his column regularly—it was a must read. He knew the pulse of the city and what was going on. He was an *authority*!

Well, Herb Caen was not only famous for writing about his beloved San Francisco, he was also famous for always taking shots at Oakland! In one column he wrote, "The trouble with Oakland is that when you get there, it's there." Can you imagine? Another time he said of Oakland: "It has one monument: a towering inferiority complex."

These comments did not sit well with me, of course! After one incident I called Herb Caen up, wanting him to come over to Oakland and see for himself all that Oakland had to offer. Somehow this ended up with him attending and speaking at an Oakland Chamber of Commerce function—and it was at this function, on February 16, 1957, that he also autographed my personal copy of his book, *Herb Caen's Guide to San Francisco*.

This book was brand-new at the time, and it was to become a key reference for me! I especially used to refer to his chapter titled "The Restaurants." In it, he described the history of dining in San Francisco and included a list of places to dine.

I dated frequently, and on my dates I usually included dinner at one of "Herb Caen's restaurants." Dining with my guest gave me the opportunity to get to know her—it was very enjoyable. I soon had my own long list of restaurants that I frequented: Alexis' Tangier, Alfred's, Amelio's, Bardelli's, Blue Fox, Blum's, Cliff House, David's Delicatessen, DiMaggio's, Domino Club, Ernie's, Exposition Fish

Grotto, Fairmont Hotel (Papagayo Room, Tonga Room, and the Venetian Room), Fior D'Italia, Gino's, Grison's Steak House, Hotel St. Francis Mural Room, Hotel Sir Francis Drake, India House, Iron Horse, Jack's, Julius' Castle, Kan's (Johnny Kan), Le Boeuf, Little Sweden, Lupo's, New Joe's, Omar Khayyam's, Owl 'n' Turtle, Paoli's, Pietro's, Piro's, Place Pigalle, Ritz Old Poodle Dog, Sam's Grill, Schroeder's, Shadows, Sheraton-Palace Hotel's Garden Court, Sorrento, Tadich Grill, Tarantino's, Tokyo Sukiyaki, Trader Vic's, Vanessi's, and Yamato Sukiyaki House.

In addition to the restaurants listed in Herb Caen's book, I would also bring my dates to Doro's (owned by Don Dianda and located next to Melvin Belli's famous law offices in North Beach), the Hungry I, Purple Onion, Il Matador, Ondine's in Sausalito, and the Sally Stanford's Valhalla in Sausalito. The entertainment at some of these places was great too: Mort Sahl was at the Hungry I, and Phyllis Diller was at the Purple Onion.

Herb Caen's book would list the prices of lunches and dinners—it's amazing now to see what the prices were back in 1957! Here are some examples from the book:

> Gino's, 401 Front Street. New York steak is $3.50, boneless squab with wild rice en casserole is $3.00, and veal scaloppini, $1.75. Fine onion soup for 25 cents and coffee, believe it or don't, for a dime.
> Sam's Grill, 374 Bush Street. The highest-priced item, broiled lobster tail, is $2.50.

The book really was my guide for my dating adventures, and I was becoming something of an expert myself. People used to call *me* for advice on what restaurant to go to. I was being asked to publish my own "Dating and Dining" guide. I may have missed a great opportunity by not doing it—but I was too busy *dating and dining*!

For a while I dated a beautiful and talented dancer from Goman's Gay Nineties and Bimbo's. Marlene and I would go out after she finished dancing, and we would go to eateries in North Beach—even bowling at midnight. Marlene showed me the secret to the "Girl in the Fish Bowl" at Bimbo's … but I'll never tell!

Great Food, Great Friends, Great Memories

I used to dine out frequently, for any occasion! My Army buddies and I would have reunions in San Francisco's North Beach, a neighborhood full of excellent Italian restaurants. We would make the rounds: Fior d'Italia, North Beach

Restaurant, Café Sport, Veneto's, and so on. Our group consisted of Dante Marcolina, Ralph Weber, Frank Terranova, Arnold Tira, Peter Armanini, Lino Bruno, and George Mortimer. Often Arnold would bring his accordion to the restaurant and play for us and the other guests. Once when we went to Veneto's to see Lino Bruno (he was the head chef there), Arnold was playing and we were having an especially happy time. Someone from Los Angeles gave us his card and asked to be invited next time!

A dining tradition started in the seventies when Charles Arolla, Bob Engle, and I formed the "Gemini Luncheon Club." We would get together in June during our birthdays and celebrate at different restaurants: Sea Wolf (now Scott's at Jack London Square in Oakland—Ray Gallagher runs a great restaurant!), Bardelli's in San Francisco, and, in recent years, the same table near the window at John's Grill in San Francisco (of *Maltese Falcon* fame!).

Dining out with some former Kaiser coworkers: Marita Inchauspe, Faye Potter (the painter), Jerry Maxwell, myself, JoAnne Kearns, and Sylvia Vlahos.
Great reunion arranged by Sylvia!

At Jack London Square there is a well-known restaurant called The Fat Lady. Bob Gannon (the head of security at Kaiser Center) and I used to go there often. The food was not only great but the fish was *fresh* and outstanding.

I will never forget the time I took Sean Maher, a business partner, to Scott's at Jack London Square for lunch. The owner, Ray Gallagher, greeted us as we were going in—he said he wanted to buy us lunch. I said that would be great, but we wanted Ray to join us! He did, and we had an interesting conversation. He had learned of my investment as a limited partner in Mac's Sports Bar & Grill at Jack London Square, and he cautioned me on how risky the restaurant business is, especially if you don't keep detailed records and control costs. He showed us a spreadsheet from Scott's that enabled him to know what it cost even for the doilies used under coffee cups—really detailed. He was really trying to help me!

As a limited partner, I later discussed my meeting with some of the other limited partners and general partners, but it was too late. Mac's Sports Bar & Grill went bankrupt! Ray was right. Poor cost control and poor management brought the restaurant down. I was very disappointed!

Chew Chew

I've always had great experiences traveling by train, and many of those experiences were in the dining car. Remember my very first train trip outside the state of California? The first night I went to the dining car, I met Vivien Leigh on her way to film *A Streetcar Named Desire*!

In more recent years I took a train to Seattle for a trip on the Canadian Railway, to Banff and Lake Louise. While we were still in California, I asked the conductor of the Southern Pacific train where the dining car was located. To my surprise, there was no dining car—just an area for machines dispensing food in *cans*! Freight was given priority over passengers. What a shame!

In Europe the railway system is superb. And on time! Think of all the energy we could save with a great railway system. One built for passengers and their enjoyment, and not just freight!

Practice 6

Use this space to write down the names of friends and acquaintances you'd like to see more often.

If you feel like you don't see friends as often as you'd like and you're always too busy to make plans, consider starting a dining tradition. Pick a specific place to meet, and then come up with a regular schedule to get together—even if it's just once a year. Write down some possibilities:

CHAPTER 7

SEE WHAT GOOD COMES FROM GETTING INVOLVED

Irene Sargent, co-chair with me on the inaugural "Christmas in Oakland" event in 1981, once said in a *Newsbreak* feature about her: "Something nice always happens to me after I do a good turn for someone." As I gave my time to promoting Kaiser and promoting Oakland, I was really finding that this was true. Through all my community involvement and volunteering, which you'll read about next, I found that being willing to give time and effort can lead not only to a sense of satisfaction and fulfillment, but to other, unforeseen perks!

Membership Rewards

Beginning in the late 1950s, I was so *happy* and *proud* to serve as a Junior Achievement adviser while with Kaiser Steel in Oakland. Junior Achievement was an organization supported by business, industry, schools, and individuals, providing teenagers with a chance to learn about business by actual practice in small "companies." These Junior Achievement "companies" would receive counsel and advice from senior business organizations, such as a local business or a civic, professional, or service group in the community.

The high school students I was involved with counseling were great and goal-oriented. What a rewarding experience to contribute to their development!

Here's another example of a rewarding experience—though rewarding in a very different way! Back in the late 1960s, I was a member of the "Oakland Jaycees," or Junior Chamber of Commerce. Well, this allowed me to be on the Miss Oakland committee—a great assignment! I was involved with all the pageant activities, including going to Santa Cruz, California, for the Miss California contest, and serving as one of the pageant escorts. The morning after the Miss California pageant, we attended a great luncheon with all the contestants from California. I was lucky to interact with such beautiful women. It was first-class!

I also became a member of the Oakland Chamber of Commerce, and my experience as a member of the Trade Club, which was promoted by the Chamber, was truly rewarding. I was the Head Trader for one year, 1971–1972, after serving in different capacities, such as Entertainment Chairman.

The Trade Club was an inexpensive way to entertain your clients and friends and provided a tremendous opportunity to interact with the people who were very involved in the Metropolitan Oakland Area. The Trade Club literature stated, "The primary purpose of your Trade Club is to provide a social and good-will organization for the Metropolitan Oakland Area and to promote a spirit of friendly cooperation among the manufacturers, wholesalers, retailers, and professional men of the area. Plan to attend." (Of course, we kept up with the times and definitely included women, recognizing their *importance*.)

Trade Club functions were held monthly. The events I was involved with were held at the Claremont Hotel in Berkeley, Goodman's at Jack London Square, and the Oakland Museum. The evening would start with a reception at 6:00 PM, followed by dinner at 7:00 PM and great entertainment at 8:00 PM—all for the price of $7.50! What a bargain. Each event would be sponsored by numerous organizations that would then receive mention in a flyer. For example, the Restaurant and Entertainment Night listed thirty-four restaurants as sponsors.

Chris Marshall, Rite Trader, who worked for the Oakland Chamber of Commerce, worked closely with me on the planning and execution of each monthly event. He was a great member of my team! We would go to dinner and discuss all the details, including what we would serve for dinner and who the entertainers would be. We took our job seriously. It was great fun, and we wanted everything to go like clockwork. We wanted people to enjoy themselves and find the experience top-notch. We wanted them to spread the word and come back and continue supporting the events!

I have a collection of party pictures that prove a great time was had by all at these events. In particular I remember the party at the end of my one-year term as Head Trader. (It was a tradition to honor the Head Trader with a wonderful party.) I was really honored by my friends! (My family!)

Sadly, the Trade Club was canceled after funding became difficult. But I think the time has come for Oakland to reactivate it—the benefits for Oakland would be wonderful!

In addition to being involved with the Chamber of Commerce, I was active in the board of directors of the East Bay's Better Business Bureau. As in the Trade Club, the members comprising this group held important positions with local and national businesses.

I was also a member of the Rotary Club of Oakland, which is Club No. 3. It is a requirement as a new member of the Rotary Club to give your life history before the membership in three minutes. So, to introduce myself I prepared a three-minute speech covering fifty years—can you imagine!

At one Rotary Club meeting, I was chosen to introduce Elaine Corrall, newscaster for the Bay Area's Channel 2. Great fun!

Miss Oakland and runners-up atop
the Kaiser Roof Garden, 1967.
Getting involved comes with perks!

When the Bay Area Rapid Transit (BART) system opened in Oakland in 1972, I was privileged to attend the official opening festivities at the Lake Merritt Station, which was the control center for the entire BART system. A lot of community leaders were there, and the celebrity guest of honor was Donald O'Connor, who I had always admired. I had my picture taken with him, which I treasure!

In addition to Oakland city organizations like the Chamber of Commerce, I enjoyed being involved with a key international business organization related to my field: BOMA International. BOMA stands for Building Owners and

Managers Association. This organization played a very important role in my career, not only relating to real estate but also to public relations and community relations. For instance, I applied for and received the designation "RPA," or Real Property Administrator, from the BOMA organization in 1978—a boost to my resume.

I was active in BOMA on a local, regional, and international level. I was President of the local chapter in Oakland for three and a half years. I was General Conference Chairman of the Pacific Southwest Regional Conference in 1974 (the first time Oakland hosted the Pacific Southwest conference). I was active as a speaker, a panelist, a moderator, a director, and in other capacities.

I was first asked to speak in 1964, at the Pacific Southwest Regional Conference. What an honor! My speech was titled "Financial Control of Contract Cleaning," and the speech later appeared in the March 1965 issue of *Skyscraper Management Magazine* with the subheading "The Science of Cost Saving."

In 1975, it was a thrill for me to be a panelist in the Pasadena Workshop where, in partnership with John N. (Pete) Dayton, President of Buckbee Thorne & Co., we role-played "The Art of Lease Negotiations."

I was also called upon year after year to give the speech, "What's New in Oakland." I would spread the good word about Oakland. I was never quiet about Oakland! "Here's 'Mr. Oakland!'" they would say when introducing me.

Benefits of belonging to BOMA included access to information and news related to our industry and business, as well as to statistics and research that could help with business planning; professional education and career development; and opportunities to interact with industry leaders. But the conventions were an especially wonderful perk of being a member of BOMA! The annual international convention would always be held in a different city in late June so that the members' families could attend after school closed for summer vacation. I want to stress the *family* relationship we promoted!

We had conventions in San Francisco; Los Angeles; San Diego; Atlanta; New Orleans; Boston; New York; Washington, D.C.; Portland, Oregon; Dallas; Vancouver, Canada; Salt Lake City; Hawaii; Chicago; and other locations. The Allied members (those companies providing services to high-rise buildings, like security companies, elevator maintenance firms, and window washing services) would always have exhibits at the conventions showcasing their products and services, and sometimes they would sponsor receptions or events.

Don and Jo Lee of Westinghouse Elevator in particular were like family. It is always great to "break bread" with your members! This was proven when Westinghouse sponsored a New England Clambake on the beach in Santa Monica. At the clambake we could mingle with BOMA members from all over the world. The waiters in tuxedos took our orders for drinks on the beach, while lobsters were being cooked in huge pots.

One of our BOMA conventions was held in Detroit in June 1980. We stayed at the Landmark Hotel Renaissance. We were able to go to Dearborn, Michigan, to visit the famous Ford Museum. Another highlight was the tour of the famous "automobile row" houses. We saw the mansions of the automobile makers. This convention also happened to coincide with an Italian festival being held next to the Renaissance. I was impressed: wonderful fun and food—Italian, of course!

During the June 1982 BOMA International Convention in Washington, D.C., our BOMA officers hosted a beautiful cocktail and buffet dinner in one of the city's landmark buildings. I treasure a memory at the party attended by Bonnie Guiton and myself. We were at the table of appetizers and I had just relished one particular appetizer. A gentleman in front of me was trying to decide what to choose. I suggested that he try the one I had just enjoyed. He tasted it and turned around to thank me for the great suggestion! I suddenly realized that this gentleman was Casper Weinberger, Secretary of Defense.

Bonnie and I had a photo taken with Mr. Weinberger, and this photo was later transmitted to me by Paul J. Hyman, Defense Department official. The letter of transmittal was included, with an offer to visit the Pentagon!

BOMA conventions were always an adventure!

After the BOMA Convention in Washington, D.C., I took four days of vacation time to tour the city. I was privileged to see the great 97th Congress in action. I had to get special visitor's passes: one for the U.S. House of Representatives, approved by Paul N. McCloskey, Jr., and one for the United States Senate Chamber, approved by Alan Cranston. I have kept these passes as souvenirs. They gave me the ability to go from the House to the Senate, and to return to the House in the early evening to witness the voting process. The guard had told me to return because there was a vote scheduled to be taken, and I would see many congressional representatives present. It was exciting! There he was: the white-haired Speaker of the House, Thomas P. "Tip" O'Neill, with his gavel to bring order to the House during the debates. Earlier, when I was in the Senate, I had seen Barry Goldwater surrounded by other senators. He was really the center of attention.

Also in Washington, D.C., I visited the Smithsonian, which has a terrific storehouse of exhibits. I attended a concert in the Mall, which was overflowing with a standing-room-only crowd. I experienced the lively nightlife in Georgetown, with its music and restaurants. Also, I toured the White House and the United States Capitol. The guides were great, and I kept the souvenir tickets. A great trip in particular was by elevator to the top of the Washington Monument. I recommend this for everyone! It was in conjunction with a conducted tour of the city and other landmarks. What a wonderful educational experience overall—it made me proud to be an American.

Another adventure I enjoyed was after the Los Angeles BOMA Convention, when Don Lee invited a few of us to ride up the coast in their Westinghouse custom trailer, to go salmon fishing in Westport, Washington. Don Lee and his lovely wife, Jo, were great hosts. We went out to where the skipper promised us we would catch our limit. You know something? He was right! I caught a salmon and brought the whole fish home to Mama. It was packed in *ice*.

In the summer of 1977 I attended a BOMA convention in New York City, which was memorable mainly because of the events that occurred on my way home! You see, at the time I was dating a nurse in San Francisco, and I had asked her what she would like me to bring back to her as a souvenir. She had replied, "Bring back live lobsters, and I will pick you up at the San Francisco Airport and cook them for us for dinner."

So, at the end of the convention in New York, I asked the Hilton desk staff where I could buy live lobsters to bring back to San Francisco. They directed me to the Fulton Fish Market, which was a great choice. I talked to a Sicilian salesman and told him of my "romantic promise." He was also a romantic, and fixed me up with two large lobsters packed in seaweed and dry ice. When I went back to the Hilton, the staff was great and put them in the hotel refrigerator for me to pick up in the morning before my return via American Airlines to San Francisco.

That evening I took a cab to Central Park to take a horse-drawn carriage ride. The driver of the carriage was Sicilian, and he wanted to know all about San Francisco and my family. He wanted me to sit next to him rather than in the back—what a treat to see Central Park from the *top* of the carriage. We talked in Sicilian, and it was marvelous. He invited me to have dinner with his family. You see, I was never alone!

The next morning I checked out and, armed with my suitcase and lobsters, I took a cab to the airport. When I boarded the plane with my lobsters, the dry ice was smoking. (Can you imagine what would happen today if I tried to board a plane with a box that was smoking?) The stewardesses were also romantics—they put the "smoking box" in their refrigerator.

My trip was wonderful, and I was looking forward to seeing my girlfriend and having a romantic lobster dinner. However, as I sat there in my window seat looking out my window, I suddenly spotted flames coming out of the right side of the plane!

I called for the stewardess, who went to the pilots. The pilots announced that we had a fire in one of the motors and to "buckle up"! Luckily they were able to maneuver the plane until the flames went out.

When we arrived in San Francisco, the pilots thanked me for being alert, and I thanked them for keeping my lobsters in the refrigerator. We joked about landing with broiled lobsters. In those days, you could joke about these things!

My girlfriend picked me up at the airport, and we went to her apartment in the Marina District. The dry ice was still smoking and the lobsters were alive! But she was so nervous about *killing* the lobsters in *boiling water*. We began to think about going out to dinner instead. Finally, she said, "I'm a nurse—I can do this." It turned out to be a great evening!

I also have fond memories of attending the BOMA convention in Portland, Oregon. The convention coincided with that city's famous Rose Parade (there is a beautiful Rose Garden in Portland), so I was able to watch the parade from the balcony of the Hilton Hotel. While watching the parade, I started up a conversation with a lovely couple next to me. They were interested to learn that I was from Oakland and representing the BOMA chapter as President. We enjoyed the conversation and the parade, and afterwards they asked me to lunch. The lunch was in honor of all the volunteers who made the parade possible!

When I arrived at the luncheon, I was escorted to the *head table* and seated next to the couple I had just met on the balcony. It turns out that the gentleman was a retired founding member of the Rose Parade festivities. He introduced me as "Mr. Oakland" and asked me to say a few words. What a wonderful surprise! I have always felt that there are wonderful people to encounter and adventures to be had—just be prepared to enjoy, and be friendly and smile!

Anytime I appeared as a panelist, gave a speech, or visited the BOMA conventions, I gained self-confidence and was able to be an "Ambassador of Oakland."

There were many benefits to belonging to BOMA, as you can see. But I want to highlight a personal benefit that gave me a great appreciation of "skyscrapers": during conventions, we were given the chance to tour major buildings in the city hosting the convention. Some buildings we toured were still under construction, like the Pyramid Building in San Francisco. (I was allowed to climb to the "tip"!) We would view the machinery rooms that provided heat and air-conditioning. The huge buildings are really like individual cities, providing for the comfort and welfare of their "citizens," or tenants. This opportunity to see them made the conventions a truly hands-on learning experience.

A BOMA brochure notes, "The first national gathering of the office building industry was held in Chicago in 1908, with 75 people attending from 26 cities. Perhaps symbolically, the first office building to be widely acclaimed as a 'sky-scraper'—the 47-story Singer Building in New York—was erected that same year. (The term 'skyscraper' originated in Chicago in 1885 with the construction of the 10-story steel-skeleton Home Life Insurance Company Building.)"

During a BOMA convention held in New York, we were invited to tour the Twin Towers of the World Trade Center. In the evening we had dinner at the top, in the Windows of the World restaurant—a memory I shall never forget!

Benefiting Others Has Its Benefits

Besides all the civic and business organizations I was involved with, I also volunteered for various charities such as the Salvation Army and the United Way. For over twenty years, I was very active in the United Way fund-raising campaigns, setting them up and so on. I was even the "Sponsored Executive of the Year" in 1975.

It was very rewarding to be involved and to be able to make a difference in the lives of so many needy individuals. I have always felt that "what goes around comes around"!

One year I was asked to participate in the Telethon for Easter Seals, which I did along with local husband-and-wife TV hosts Fred LaCosse and Terry Lowry. My job was to answer phones along with some other volunteers, and since I was well-known in the community the announcers would sometimes focus the camera on me and say things like, "There's John Rubino—give him a call!"

In 1987, Noreen Quan and I co-chaired the "You Gotta Have Heart" Gala Auction Dinner Dance, which was sponsored by the Heart Lung Institute of the East Bay. This was an elegant affair, held at the Hyatt Regency in Oakland.

Noreen was a marvelous co-chairperson. Kathleen Cassidy made everything flow with her guidance to us, and Dr. Ivan May gave us *inspirational* support. It was such a worthwhile project. Funds from "You Gotta Have Heart" were used to help establish one of the first community-based heart and lung replacement programs.

The biggest volunteer project I ever took on, which you'll read about next, also resulted in some very big rewards—not the least of which was the satisfaction of having done it! Just try to imagine the scope:

On June 21, 1983, the Oakland City Council passed Resolution No. 61477 C.M.A., extending appreciation and congratulations to the volunteers, staff, and professionals who together made dedication of the Oakland Convention Center/George P. Scotlan Memorial an outstanding and overwhelming success. This official document states:

> Resolved: That the City Council extends appreciation and congratulations to John Rubino, General Chairman, and to all the volunteers, staff, and professionals who joined together to make the Dedication Ceremonies and "Showcase Oakland" an historic day for the City of Oakland.

Whereas the planning of this event was undertaken by approximately 150 volunteers donating their time and expertise over a nine-month period …"

Can you imagine: 150 volunteers! The dedication ceremonies and "Showcase Oakland" was a three-day event meant to inform people of the new Convention Center, and also showcase the diverse resources, talent, and services available in Oakland. The fun started with a parade, and then inside the Convention Center we had nonstop entertainment: big-league sports teams and players; about thirty-eight different musical or dance groups performing (from Brazilian dancers to gospel groups, and from opera singers to local school bands); three-hundred pieces of art on display, including locally produced films being shown; and booths showcasing the products and services of local businesses. It took months to plan the event, with seventeen committees in all handling various facets of the production, from entertainment to food to signage to transportation and security. And I was the person in charge!

This was an incredible event, and so rewarding since I was able to work with the entire community. I was so fortunate to have Dianne Lichtenstein as my assistant. She was terrific! I got a feel for what it would be like to be Mayor of Oakland. In fact, after these dedication ceremonies were over and had been a huge success, I was being referred to as "Mr. Oakland" and people were saying I should consider running for Mayor. Stay tuned!

One year after the success of "Showcase Oakland" and the dedication ceremonies, I was privileged to be named Honorary Chairman of the "Festival at the Lake," June 1–3, 1984, along with Chairman of the Festival Bill Garvine. Located in Lakeside Park, Lake Merritt, Oakland, this festival was the East Bay's second annual urban fair, featuring exhibitions, performances, competitions, parades, and demonstrations of dance, music, arts, and food. It was open to the public free of charge.

Of course, at this event I was exactly one year older—and definitely one year wiser. You see, this was a time when some very surprising changes were occurring in my career. And the long list of community and public relations activities I had been involved with—and the people I met through these activities—would soon make all the difference!

Practice 7

Make a list of civic and business organizations you may be eligible to join. For instance, is there a trade group related to your line of work? Find out what organizations are available locally and nationally, and consider how it may benefit you to join.

Next, make a list of charities or similar organizations that do work you can appreciate. Make another list of the skills you have to contribute. If you need to start small, consider setting aside just one day or a few hours of your time to volunteer, and see how it makes you feel to get involved.

CHAPTER 8

HE REALLY DOES OPEN A WINDOW (PART 2)

Remember how in 1952 I received the bad news that I was being drafted during the Korean Conflict—and yet what I thought was bad news actually turned out to be a great opportunity? In 1983, I was about to learn the same lesson about hidden blessings again.

Graduation Day

The 1980s started off with a bang for me, with the success of Kaiser Airline Center, the opening of the Convention Center, and so on in that vein. In 1983, I was privileged to take not one but *two* trips to Hawaii, during which I met with David Stringer, the architect working on Kaiser's Oakland Master Plan, an ongoing plan for the expansion of the property around Kaiser Center. (I made the first trip specifically to meet with the architect, and the second trip to Hawaii was for the annual BOMA convention, after which I along with other key executives met with the architect again.)

These expansion plans the architect was working on were part of continual expansion that was in line with Henry J. Kaiser's vision, and we as employees were always working toward accomplishing them. For instance, each year I would receive yearly goals, and typically some of the goals were directly related to the company's expansion. As far back as 1970, Frank Scarr issued a program of goals for the year that outlined our expansion program and other real estate accomplishments, and included instruction to me to lease the new Ordway Building. In 1969, I made a speech to the Kiwanis Club regarding the Ordway Building, and referred to the acquisition of other properties adjacent to our Kaiser Center to cover long-range needs for future expansion. In that speech I also quoted Henry Kaiser, who famously said: "We can, if we will, keep forever building the tomorrow that is better than yesterday."

By 1983, the plans in the works for the site around Kaiser Center were impressive, including four new towers and two new garden levels—in all the development of about six million square feet of space! It was an exciting time.

And then a few months after the June BOMA convention in Hawaii and meeting with the Master Plan architect again, the unthinkable happened. The

Kaiser Empire was in trouble, and I received notice that my position had been eliminated!

I never thought that this would happen. Imagine my disbelief as I wrote this memo on November 23, 1983:

> To: Administrative Committee, Salaried Benefits Administration
> The Company has notified me that my position has been eliminated and that I will be eligible for a full early retirement effective February 29, 1984. In lieu of 90 days notice, I request that my retirement date be effective December 31, 1983.
> Signed, John M. Rubino

Fortunately I had almost twenty-eight years' service and was entitled to a full retirement pension and benefits, including medical. Bonnie Guiton, our Vice President and General Manager, and Tim Preece, our President, were very supportive in allowing me full early retirement. In addition, effective immediately upon my retirement, they hired me as a consultant to handle the leasing and tenant relations for remaining properties! This was a blessing in itself—though there was much more to come.

In talking to Tim Preece and Bonnie Guiton, I realized we were all saddened at the upheaval of our plans for expansion. In fact, now the opposite of expansion was occurring! Various Kaiser companies were being sold; even the Ordway Building would be sold—on December 30, 1983, one day before my retirement.

Remember, we had just been to Hawaii for the BOMA convention and to discuss Kaiser's expansion. At the BOMA convention, which was held June 4, 1983 (my birthday), I gave the talk, "What's New in Oakland"—setting a positive tone as usual! Bonnie Guiton and John McClure were also there, and we had had a very productive meeting with the architect.

It was so painful to realize later on that the Master Plan was not going ahead.

The *San Francisco Chronicle* published a number of articles on Henry J. Kaiser and Edgar Kaiser, providing insight into what happened to the Kaiser Empire. The articles speculated on what may have brought it to this point: the recession, for one thing, and Kaiser Steel and other heavy industries were having to compete with foreign imports, which enjoyed government subsidies and other help that Kaiser companies did not. There was also speculation that after World War II, the company just did not change to meet the changing times.

As I said earlier, Tim and Bonnie were both great to me during this time. To celebrate my retirement, Tim took me to Mirabeau Restaurant for a memorable lunch. After lunch, he told me that he wanted to take me to dinner at a later date.

A few weeks later, Tim called and asked me to meet him at the Blue Fox Restaurant—a famous top-notch restaurant in San Francisco. When I arrived, the valet took my car. Inside, Tim greeted me and introduced me to the manager, who said he wanted to take me on a tour of the facilities, including the private dining rooms. They took me downstairs to the Cellar (a wine cellar dining room). The manager opened the two large doors, and all of a sudden I heard, *"Surprise!"* It was the Kaiser Center staff with their husbands and wives. Here I had thought that Tim was going to have dinner with me alone. What a wonderful night—this was my *family*!

But that wasn't the end of my retirement celebrations. At the office, our Kaiser Center employees threw another surprise party! They had a beautiful cake with a rainbow, presents, hugs and kisses—what a wonderful time.

Later, when I was already working for her as a consultant, Bonnie Guiton called me into her office and informed me that she wanted to have a party that the City of Oakland could attend. She said that since I was "Mr. Oakland" and had participated in so many activities, we must invite the people of Oakland to participate. She said it was only fitting that the event should be held at the Mirabeau Restaurant overlooking the Roof Garden, and my family should join me in this honor.

And what an honor it was! The invitation read "Santa Goes into Retirement," referencing all the years I had played Santa Claus for the Christmas festivities. The guest list was impressive, including almost three hundred invitees! Among these were community leaders, tenants, and Kaiser employees. And Bonnie Guiton, Tim Preece, and Mayor Lionel Wilson not only attended but also spoke about my Kaiser and community involvement.

My Mama and family were also at the party, of course—my mother was so *proud* and was beaming. I was so proud of her! *I was truly thankful to God for this occasion, as I was able to share it with my family.*

The party included a great buffet planned and prepared by Andre Mercier, Chef and General Manager of the Mirabeau. Attendees wrote special messages in a keepsake book, and many wonderful pictures were taken. Other invitees wrote me cards or letters even if they couldn't attend, including Dean Grether from UC Berkeley. Burton Weber, of the City of Oakland's Office of Parks and Recreation, wrote me an especially beautiful letter that I enjoy to this day.

God has been so *kind* to me! I addressed the crowd and said that I was honored by everybody being there, and I thanked them for helping me along the way. I said that this day, March 26, 1984, was really my "Graduation Day." I felt something promising was in store for me. As it turns out, I was right!

SANTA Goes Into Retirement!

He made Oakland's holidays brighter . . . was chairman of Dedication Ceremonies for the Oakland Convention Center . . . he was even a Rhinestone Cowboy for the A's Western Night!

After 28 years of dedicated service to Kaiser Center, Inc. and the Oakland Community, JOHN RUBINO is retiring.

Please join us at John's retirement party.

WHEN: Monday, March 26, 1984 - 5:00 - 7:00 p.m.

WHERE: Mirabeau Restaurant
344 20th Street
Oakland, CA 94612

COST: $12.00 per person
(includes hors d'oeuvres, wine, soft drinks and your gift contribution)

Return your reservation and check NO LATER than Friday, March 16th. Make your checks payable to M. INCHAUSPE (no cash, please).

The wonderful invitation to my retirement party.

Top: Bonnie Guiton, my Mama, and me at my retirement party—my graduation!
Bottom: Tim Preece, Mayor Lionel Wilson, Mama, and me.

Another Silver Lining

As I mentioned earlier, Bonnie Guiton hired me as a consultant in 1984, effective upon my retirement in December 1983. This itself was a blessing, but it also provided me with an opportunity of a lifetime!

While I was working as a consultant, Jerry Lewis, Manager of the Cushman & Wakefield office located in the Ordway Building, got in touch with me. He wanted me to locate additional space in the Ordway Building, because he needed to establish an office that would handle marketing for the new Pankow Building, a twenty-story, 500,000-square-foot office tower developed by Charles Pankow, to be built at 2101 Webster in Oakland. (I was still involved with the Ordway Building because its new owners had hired Kaiser Center, Inc.—and thus me as a consultant—to continue handling property management and leasing.)

After finding an ideal location with Jerry, I invited him to the Mirabeau for lunch. We had a great conversation—he was especially interested in my many community activities. Then Jerry told me that since I had a lot of expertise in leasing and marketing the Kaiser and Ordway buildings in Oakland, Cushman & Wakefield needed me to be their listing broker for the Pankow Building!

I was flattered, naturally—but I mentioned to Jerry that I had a very favorable consulting contract with Kaiser Center. However, Jerry called me a few days later and said he wanted me to meet with the President of Cushman & Wakefield, John Renard, in John's offices in the Bank of America Center in San Francisco. I told Bonnie Guiton of this overture, and she said I had her blessing to look into it!

What an exciting and rewarding experience. I was very impressed in meeting John Renard—he was *enthusiastic* and a great marketing mentor! He wouldn't take no for an answer, and we negotiated a very, very favorable arrangement for me. So I reported back to Bonnie! She said to accept the offer, as it was wonderful for my career.

So I "graduated" to Cushman & Wakefield, a commercial real estate firm. It turned out to be a great decision on my part! *The right road taken.*

My title at Cushman & Wakefield was Vice President and Director of Marketing and Promotion. After I was hired, Cushman & Wakefield issued in its public relations newsletter a news item about me titled "Meet Cushman & Wakefield's Ambassador of Goodwill in Oakland." What a great article! Michaele Ballard, the editor, perfectly captured my history in Oakland: "The new director of marketing for the Oakland office has worked in the community with Kaiser Center for 28 years. But more importantly is the hundreds of hours he has logged in the community promoting Oakland—its people, its businesses and its potential." The article finished with: "Every time John Rubino extends his hand in an introduction, leaves his calling card, or takes on a new community project, Oakland is introduced to Cushman & Wakefield."

As predicted, Cushman & Wakefield was awarded the listing for the Pankow Building, and I was appointed the listing broker.

The adventure begins! Handling this building at 2101 Webster started off a very exciting and financially rewarding chapter in my life. As the Project Manager for the Pankow Building, I coordinated all the leasing and promotion activities for the four-person brokerage team established for the project. I selected Jeff Smith to be on my team, who acted as my right-hand assistant. He proved to be a great friend and a great salesman!

Our team set up a "Marketing Center" for 2101 Webster in the Ordway Building and set to work. Mike Townsend of Pankow Development was a terrific supporter of our efforts. He was also active in the community and understood my vision for the marketing success of 2101.

Charles Pankow, the developer of 2101 Webster, lived in a magnificent mansion in San Francisco called "Le Petit Trianon." I was privileged to be invited to a Christmas party there while I was responsible for marketing the 2101 building in Oakland. Charles Pankow took me on a personal tour of his mansion, which included Egyptian antiquities and other great artworks. I still remember the white grand piano where we all gathered and sang holiday songs. What an event!

Charles Pankow thanked me for my imaginative marketing techniques and my emphasis on *providing adequate parking*. The parking problem around 2101 Webster was solved with the building of a multilevel garage on Broadway not too far from 2101. In developing the Broadway site to provide parking, Pankow also made a tax-deductible donation by including a beautiful new home for the YMCA. In the nine-story mixed-use building, six stories were for parking, and three were for the YMCA. I had direct contact with the YMCA officials and I had promoted this "partnership." It was so rewarding—in this type of deal, everybody wins!

One of the first deals I made in my new role at Cushman & Wakefield was not only full of drama and excitement, but also the biggest deal of that year in Oakland! Here is the story of the famous Blue Cross drama.

Blue Cross of Northern California had its headquarters in Oakland and was a big employer there. But in the early 1980s, the Northern California Blue Cross merged with its Southern California division. Then in 1984, Blue Cross sold its company headquarters building in Oakland to the Kaiser Foundation Health Plan. Word got out that Blue Cross was moving out of Oakland, and pretty soon its employees were up in arms, demonstrating before the Mayor and the City Council!

At this time we had a lot of space still to lease in 2101 Webster—which was just a block away from the previous Blue Cross headquarters. So, recognizing an opportunity, I enlisted the help of the Chamber of Commerce president, Bill Downing, to put the word out that 2101 would be perfect for Blue Cross.

The broker working for Blue Cross introduced the building to them as an option. However, we soon learned we had our work cut out for us: the president of Blue Cross was rumored to have said, "Don't talk to me about 2101," complaining that the building felt "squished."

But here's where not taking no for an answer pays off! I next called Tom Davies, a Senior Vice President at Blue Cross, whom I knew from Rotary Club. I took him to lunch and he revealed some internal politics: among Blue Cross decision-makers, one faction wanted to move to Los Angeles, while the rest wanted to remain in Oakland. (No wonder Blue Cross ultimately looked at twenty-eight buildings and took eighteen months to find a new home!)

Tom agreed to take a tour of 2101, and afterwards he said he was impressed with the building. He then told me that he might become more involved with the selection of Blue Cross's new headquarters building, and that if so he would suggest 2101 despite the president's dislike of it.

After our promising meeting, however, any deal with Blue Cross began to seem unlikely. This is because we learned that the president of Blue Cross wanted to buy a building rather than lease space. However, the owner of the building he wanted to buy was proving difficult, and the deal between Blue Cross and the building owner was an on-again, off-again situation. I remained a "friendly pest," continually reminding them about 2101 Webster ... until finally Blue Cross agreed to an official tour!

The plan was for Blue Cross's broker to bring Roy Heinberger, a Senior Vice President and Financial Officer, from Southern California to see the building, along with some other Blue Cross executives. Our team brainstormed how to best make this deal happen. I knew I wanted to stress "visualization." The real estate market was extremely competitive and you couldn't waste time—you had to use *imagination* in making deals.

I arranged to have Russ Osterman, the President of Pankow Development, fly up from Altadena in Southern California and join us as we toured the floors. This was an eye-opening experience for him: When he saw that some of the lower floors had a view overlooking the brick wall of an adjacent building, he turned and said quietly to me, "These floors are terrible—we have got to make this deal!"

At the conclusion of the tour and presentation, Jeff Smith and I revealed the pièce de résistance: we had made a 3-by-3-foot poster with the Blue Cross logo superimposed on the parapet of the 2101 Webster building. During our presentation, the poster had sat on a tripod off to the side, with a cover over it. When the presentation to the executives was over, we walked them to the easel and said, "In conclusion, we'd like you to take this memento of your visit today to help you visualize what the Pankow Building would mean to you." Then we unveiled the poster and handed it to them, so they walked away with an image of the building with a Blue Cross sign at the top. We wanted to help Blue Cross visualize themselves in the building!

After the tour, I kept in touch with Tom Davies, and with another Blue Cross contact I knew through BOMA. I also encouraged Russ Osterman to keep in contact with Roy Heinberger. It all paid off: in December 1985, at the Blue Cross Christmas party, we signed the deal! Blue Cross leased ten of the building's twenty floors—half the building—in a $40 million deal.

Jim McPhee also played a key role in assisting me with the Blue Cross deal and with a deal to rent some of the remaining space in 2101 to Touche Ross. Jim and I later made a speech before Cushman & Wakefield brokers about the drama and sheer excitement surrounding both deals. Real estate is a *great profession*!

The next very rewarding project was Lake Merritt Plaza. My involvement with this beautiful building began when Shurl Curci, the owner of Transpacific Development Company (TDC) of Torrance, California, approached me at a black-tie affair celebrating its official opening. He said he was impressed with my success at 2101 Webster, and that he would like me to market Lake Merritt Plaza!

A few days later, Peter Adams, President of TDC, met with me and John Renard, President of Cushman & Wakefield, and our branch manager, Rich Larsen. Peter requested that I become the exclusive leasing agent for Lake Merritt. John Renard was overjoyed, and accepted the offer on an official basis. You see, this was unusual to have business come in so effortlessly. Typically Cushman & Wakefield would have to approach a building owner and make a formal proposal in an effort to win the leasing contract!

I selected Jeff Smith and Audrey Shimkas to make up our talented team, and then we issued a marketing letter to my many contacts in the community and real estate field, announcing our team and the Plaza itself. "Meet me at the Plaza," it said—and this became our marketing theme. We developed a whole marketing program from there, highlighting the building's attractive design and location and its many amenities.

Lake Merritt Plaza turned out to be a marvelous experience. I enjoyed going to work every day! Susan Munday and Bill Cutler, representing TDC, were fantastic to work with. We were truly a *team*! For instance, in addition to all our marketing efforts at Cushman & Wakefield, TDC instituted an "instant commission" program that was very clever. This encouraged brokers from around the Bay Area to bring their clients to Lake Merritt Plaza first, because if the client chose to lease space at the Plaza, the broker would receive 50 percent of his or her commission instantly. (Normally it takes months and months after signing a deal, sometimes even a year, before a broker sees any money.)

Naturally, Jeff Smith and I received the first "instant commission" check, and got our picture taken (all smiles!) with Susan Munday in the Plaza's internal newsletter.

Jeff Smith, Susan Munday, and myself promoting TDC's "instant commission" program, with Jeff and me accepting the first instant commission check. Notice Kaiser Center in the background, and beautiful Lake Merritt Plaza behind my left shoulder. (Photo © Olof Källström)

Sean Maher was another terrific real estate partner. We worked not only with Lake Merritt Plaza but with other projects in Oakland. He had a great personality and business flair.

After our team had leased a substantial amount of the space in Lake Merritt Plaza, I was very proud to receive a letter from the President of TDC. This letter indicated that the Plaza had been able to obtain permanent financing, and that the institution providing the loan had based its decision largely on the value of the leases and the credibility of the tenants—"which," he wrote, "you played an instrumental part in obtaining." How rewarding. Like I said, real estate is a great profession!

The next adventure and challenge was the exclusive listing assignment of 1800 Harrison. This building had lost a major tenant—American President Lines—

when that company's lease expired and they decided to move to the new City Center project.

I selected Mike Bernatz and Dan Harvey to assist me. I knew that under the extremely competitive marketing conditions in Oakland, we would have to try to get a large user for the space and "make an offer that they could *not* refuse!"

I had had dealings with various Kaiser Foundation Health Plan executives and employees, having leased space to them before and also interacting with them in the business community. There was often talk around this time of how their business was growing ... so while we were coming up with ideas for 1800 Harrison, I had a gut feeling that Kaiser was thinking of expanding and that this would be a perfect fit for them!

At this time, I was President of Oakland's BOMA chapter, so as President I contacted the BOMA member Dave Van Noy, who represented Kaiser Foundation Health Plan, and invited him to tour the building before I showed it to other prospects. He agreed, and after this tour and meeting, on August 6, 1991, I received a letter of authorization from Joe Colbath, Real Estate Area Manager of Kaiser Foundation, to represent them for the 1800 Harrison building! It turns out they had just recently hired a broker from another brokerage firm to locate a new space for them in Oakland, and here I was bringing a great space to their attention. You see how *timing* is so important!

But the deal-making was far from over. "Office politics" entered into our negotiations with Kaiser Foundation. And wouldn't you know it: Blue Cross was adding to the drama for us again! Here's what happened.

Blue Cross had by now decided to move *out* of their space at 2101 Webster and sublease the space to another tenant. Another broker in our Cushman & Wakefield office was representing their sublease space at 2101 Webster, and Kaiser Foundation was considering this space too. This other Cushman & Wakefield broker had his office right next to mine, and here we were competing against each other to lease space to Kaiser Foundation!

Well, the "walls were thin" as they say, and I suspected that he could hear my team and me discussing rental rates and strategy. So, we made it a point for him to hear about our "high" rental rate offer to Kaiser Foundation. We knew he would encourage Blue Cross to make an offer just under ours, because they really wanted to unload their sublease space. But of course what we made sure he overheard was a rental rate that was higher than the rate we really offered to Kaiser Foundation!

Furthermore, we had encouraged Kaiser Foundation to make a realistic appraisal of their office requirement and to protect themselves for future expansion. (The space at 1800 Harrison was larger than Blue Cross's sublease space and would allow them to expand.)

Our "office strategy" worked! Blue Cross's offer was higher than ours, and they could not accommodate the full space requirement that Kaiser Foundation had determined that they needed. So we won! Kaiser Foundation leased 219,220 square feet in the 1800 Harrison building.

In real estate every deal is different, and timing is everything! You must know the market and your competition. Our team took this into consideration—and we played the game!

Assisting us also was a broker from Coldwell Banker, Bill Walsh. He brought other tenants to our building. He displayed wonderful style and professionalism. He was great to work with, and we have shared many great Italian lunches!

This is just a sampling of the exciting deals I was privileged to take part in during my almost ten years with Cushman & Wakefield. My time there was a great experience, both for the actual work and for the many perks, like meeting and interacting with people in the business community, attending events, and traveling for conferences.

In 1986, I got to attend Cushman & Wakefield's Annual Sales Meeting conference in Palm Springs—and I received a wonderful boost to my ego along with the trip. That year, I fell short of qualifying for the meeting by a few thousand dollars (you had to have earned a certain amount to qualify for the conference), but the Oakland branch manager, Rich Larsen, wrote a memo to John Renard arguing for an exception to the policy so that I could attend. He argued:

> John is a true team player and will sacrifice commission dollars in his pocket for the betterment of the team. If you researched John's performance I am certain you would agree that he has been more than generous in co-oping all of his deals with various other agents in the office. He has that unique quality of being an unselfish professional who puts other people's interests and feelings above his own, many times a sacrifice to himself.

John Renard readily agreed, and I was able to attend the conference—plus I have this wonderful memo as a memento!

After attending the Palm Springs event, I was determined to qualify for future annual sales meetings—and it happened the very next year, when I was eligible due to my strong sales production! Lucky for me, the 1987 corporate-wide sales meeting was held in *Hawaii* at the Turtle Bay Hilton and Country Club, April 3–7. I was associating with the top producers from our firm, from all over the United States, as well as with regional managers, branch managers, and top executives. We attended conferences and social activities in beautiful Hawaii. I will treasure the experience forever!

Later, in 1992, the company was no longer holding these types of annual sales meetings. However, I received a letter from Arthur Mirante, President and CEO of Cushman & Wakefield in New York, stating, "Congratulations on your superior performance during 1991. In a year when both the U.S. real estate market and the economy hit bottom, you distinguished yourself amongst your peers." The letter went on to congratulate me on being one of the "Top 100" producers nationwide for that year. My name was inscribed on a plaque, and the company issued press releases and advertised the accomplishment in local media.

During my years as a Cushman & Wakefield broker, I also continued promoting Oakland, making speeches, and learning about and sharing what I learned regarding motivation and visualization.

In 1988, Blair Egli, the Senior Vice President and Manager of the Regional Banking Center located at the Oakland Main Office, asked me to give a speech on selling and motivation. Bank of America was starting a new policy of having their employees sell various services available, and he wanted to instill in his employees the skills involved in selling.

My assistant, Jeff Smith, shared the morning presentation with me, and Susan Munday, Lake Merritt Plaza's Marketing Director, was a great guest and gave me a lot of support. My topics were: (1) Smile. (2) Sell Others As You Would Be Sold. (3) Be Enthusiastic. (4) Set Goals. (5) Visualize Success. (6) Give Service and Find a Need and Fill It. (7) Be Loyal. (8) Close the Sale—Ask for the Order. I had done years of personal research on the topics of motivation and visualization, so I was able to include a lot of concrete examples, entertaining little stories, even a poem by Edgar Guest.

Afterwards, Blair sent me a wonderful letter of thank you, calling it an "outstanding presentation!" He wrote, "The staff continues to discuss your interesting and motivating ideas. I've already seen an improvement on the part of several employees."

Throughout my career with Cushman & Wakefield, I continued to work in Oakland even though I lived in Daly City, which is just south of San Francisco. As I had done each day for years, I would drive back and forth across the Bay Bridge to work. (In those days I was driving "against the traffic"—in the morning, for instance, more people were driving to San Francisco than were driving to Oakland.) So on the notorious date of Tuesday, October 17, 1989, I headed home after a normal workday, unaware that the Loma Prieta Earthquake would soon hit the San Francisco Bay Area, at 5:04 PM! This deadly, magnitude 7.1

earthquake would crush the freeways in Oakland and even cause a portion of the Bay Bridge upper deck to collapse.

I remember the experience vividly. At 4:30 PM, I was in my office in Oakland, finalizing a meeting with a client. Everyone else had already left the office, so I decided to drive home to watch the big game: two local teams, the San Francisco Giants and the Oakland A's, were scheduled to play the third game of the World Series at Candlestick Park at 7:00 PM.

I merged onto the Oakland freeway system leading to the Bay Bridge, then went through the toll plaza and began to cross over to San Francisco on the upper deck of the Bay Bridge. I didn't realize that *minutes* would be a matter of life and death for me!

As I descended the bridge on the San Francisco side, I noticed that my car was wobbling as if I had a flat tire. I kept on driving to get off the bridge and get to the side of the freeway in San Francisco. However, after a while the "wobbling" stopped, so I just continued on my drive home to Westlake in Daly City.

When I drove up to my house, I was greeted by my neighbors, who were all standing outside watching a battery-operated television on the hood of a car. I got out of my car wondering what was going on, and they said, "John, the Bay Bridge collapsed!" I couldn't believe it—I had just been on the bridge. I had not had my radio on, so I didn't even know there was an earthquake!

But God had been with me all the way. The freeway system in Oakland that I had been driving on minutes before had collapsed, crushing cars and killing several people. And the upper deck of the bridge did in fact collapse in a significant portion, and cars and people fell down onto the lower level. It was a catastrophe!

I had arrived home by about 5:20 PM. By mere minutes, I had missed becoming a casualty of this deadly earthquake. The Marina District in San Francisco was in flames. Many bridges and buildings were affected; it was truly a major disaster. But I was not alone—God had guided me home!

In 1993 I stopped commuting daily to Oakland: I decided to retire from Cushman & Wakefield. I decided to retire even though I had learned that I was in line to become manager of the San Jose branch. (Can you imagine? I would have been manager of a commercial real estate office during the late-nineties tech boom in Silicon Valley! I would have made millions.) But this time I was really ready to be retired. I wanted to spend time with my Mama, who was now in her nineties and needing more care. And my nine years with Cushman & Wakefield allowed me to do that comfortably—even without the potential millions that I passed up. What a blessing!

Celebrating Mama's ninetieth birthday are (clockwise beginning from front left): Joe Torrise; my great-nephew Justin; my brother's wife, Pat; my niece Josette; my nephew Bob's date; Bob; my other great-nephew Dominic; Josette's husband, Jeff; me; Mama; Marianna's husband, Pete; my nephew Ron; Marianna; Joe; and my niece Gina. In the corner is an autographed letter and photograph to my Mama from George H. W. and Barbara Bush!

Practice 8

Write about a setback you experienced recently or are going through right now. Consider how it may be a blessing in disguise, and visualize the sort of opportunities that could come of the situation.

CHAPTER 9

BE FRIENDLY, AND YOU'LL FIND FRIENDS WHEREVER YOU GO

It's probably clear by now that I enjoy meeting new friends, whether at home or abroad. And it really isn't that hard to do! Connections come about naturally when you are friendly and respectful, and show interest in others. Today I have wonderful friends all over the world—in fact, my Christmas card list has quite an "international flavor" to it. As I've said before, even though I've traveled solo for much of my life, I was never really alone!

From Coal Miners to Celebrities

You may recall that when I first started working for Kaiser Steel as an accountant back in the 1950s, I used to have to travel to Sunnyside, Utah, to deliver paychecks to the miners down in the mine. Well, funny story:

Around this time, my friends and I used to socialize at the Zanzibar, a tropical-setting cocktail lounge on Ocean Avenue in San Francisco. When the bartender, Lee, heard that I would be traveling to Sunnyside for work, he told me that his brother worked at Sunnyside as a coal miner, and if I saw him to tell him how Lee was doing!

Sunnyside was a small "company town" for the coal miners, and to get there I flew first to Salt Lake City and then to Price, which was the largest city just outside Sunnyside. Once I got to the mine site, I had to go down into the "rooms" of the mine. (Rooms were what they called individual areas within the coal mine.) My mission was to hand the paychecks to the coal miners, so that I could make sure that an actual living, working person was receiving each check.

I want to take a moment to say I was touched to see these men making a living "down under." Their faces were blackened by the coal dust. You can imagine how my visiting the mine to deliver paychecks could have been a polarized, white-collar vs. blue-collar situation.

However, when I came across Lee's brother, I handed him his paycheck—then told him that Lee in San Francisco sent his best regards! He was so surprised, and I made a friend! You know, when I can put a human face on an auditing function, it makes the job that much more meaningful. (Especially satisfying was when I later told Lee that I had met his brother in the mine and that he also sent his best.)

While we were talking in the mine, Lee's brother gave me some chewing tobacco. (You can't smoke in the mines because of the danger of igniting gases, so the miners all chewed tobacco.) Well, I started chewing and, not realizing that you are supposed to spit the tobacco juice out, I swallowed it and choked! The miners got a big kick out of me. Then all of a sudden we heard someone yell "Fire!" and we ran to another room until we got the all-clear signal. I thanked God for all of us! What an experience I will never forget.

Another unforgettable experience occurred around this time on a trip to Las Vegas. I used to enjoy going to Las Vegas regularly—in fact, I used to drive there and stay for about five days, and then drive back home to San Francisco. It used to take me about twelve hours each way.

One of my early trips was when I stayed at the Sands Hotel before it was torn down for their new tower hotel. The Sands was famous for the Rat Pack: Frank Sinatra, Dean Martin, Sammy Davis, Jr., and Joey Bishop.

In those early years, the Sands had individual cottage-type rooms around small pools. One afternoon I was at a pool and started a conversation with a beautiful lady. She had *class*. After talking with me for about a half hour, she told me she had to go get ready—for her performance at the Sands Theatre! I admitted that I was not aware of her act. She said that she would be singing, and invited me to be her guest that evening. I agreed to go, of course!

When I arrived at the theater, the head waiter told me that *Marguerite Piazza* had reserved a special table for me. I told him how thrilled I was to have met such a talented and famous personality! Marguerite Piazza was an opera singer who also appeared sometimes on TV shows like the *Dean Martin Show*, singing not only opera but also popular songs.

Marguerite's show was terrific, and my view of it was first-rate! What a marvelous voice—a real gift from God. Louis Armstrong was a headliner on her show, and he was terrific too! Marguerite really provided me with a great table.

I had told Marguerite at the time she invited me that I would like to take her to dinner after the show. She had said yes, and to meet her in the Sands Lounge area. So, after the show I went to the Lounge to wait for Marguerite. After a short time, I heard someone call out, "Giovanni!" (Johnny). It was Marguerite! She was dressed beautifully. She suggested we visit there in the Lounge before dinner. Then she called someone over to join us—it was Louis Armstrong! Imagine what a treat: talking with Marguerite and Louis Armstrong—I will cherish this memory forever. Later on, I had dinner with Marguerite and another woman who was her manager (and also her cousin, I believe).

A few years later, I got a call at my office in Kaiser Center—it was Marguerite Piazza! She invited me to her show at the Venetian Room in the Fairmont Hotel in San Francisco, and I jumped at the opportunity.

After the show I invited her to have lunch with me in Sausalito the next day. She agreed, and the next day I picked her, along with her cousin/manager, up at the Fairmont and gave them a tour of San Francisco, then drove to Sausalito for lunch. Marguerite thanked me, and for many years she would send me a Christmas card from Memphis with a picture of her *beautiful family*. In addition to being a successful performer, she and her husband had six children! What a remarkable lady.

I have encountered a few other celebrities in my life and found them to be warm and friendly as well. For instance, in the 1970s, Mama and I attended the San Mateo County Fair in the city of San Mateo. As we were walking, I recognized the famous actress Lauren Bacall. I approached her and told her how much we enjoyed her movies. She thanked us and introduced us to *her* mother. The four of us chatted for a few minutes, and after the meeting she gave me a kiss on the cheek! A great experience from a *very* classy lady.

I had another celebrity encounter when I went on a business trip to Cabo San Lucas with the Bramalea Company, a big investor in the City Center complex in Oakland. One afternoon I was near the pool, and I recognized Joe Montana (the great 49er quarterback!) with his lovely wife, Jennifer, and their two small children. Joe was teaching the children how to swim. We started a great conversation about football and about Jennifer's outstanding contribution as commentator on the *Evening Magazine* TV program. They were so friendly and natural!

I saw them again at the airport when we were all on our way back to San Francisco. Joe's private charter plane had been delayed, so we all had a chance to chat again. Great memory!

International Relations

You may recall the "Spain by Bus" trip I took while stationed in Austria in 1954—when I made numerous international friends, and one friend in particular by the name of Gigi! Well, after I got settled back in the United States, I corresponded with Gigi to let her know how I was adjusting. Naturally, I tried to convince her to come to the United States. However, Gigi was attached to Switzerland and her wonderful family. Likewise, I was busy trying to complete my education and start my business career. We shared our experiences! She eventually wrote to me that she had met a wonderful Swiss gentleman and they were getting married.

Every Christmas since, Gigi and René Bopp have sent me a Christmas card with a message, and I also do the same. We have remained the best of friends! In addition, Gigi's brother and his lovely bride came to San Francisco for their honeymoon in the mid-1960s, and I took them on a sightseeing tour of San

Francisco. Now they also exchange Christmas cards with me! It is wonderful to have friendships that last a lifetime.

Top: Gigi's brother, Pierre; his new bride;
and me in San Francisco in the 1960s.
Bottom: Pierre and me sharing a toast.

In the summer of 1970, when I turned forty, I decided to revisit Europe on a vacation, departing Saturday, July 11 and returning on August 9—almost one whole month. I arranged my trip through the California State Automobile Association's Worldwide Travel Department. The travel agent, Vivian Chastain, was great! She prepared my itinerary, helping me to save money for sightseeing, food, and so on by booking me in value-priced hotels. For instance, in Florence, Italy, she arranged for me to stay at the Plaza Lucchesi Hotel for $14 a night. This included *three meals,* and my room had a balcony overlooking Florence!

When Gigi and René learned of my upcoming trip, they insisted they would meet me at the airport in Geneva. So on July 12, Gigi, René, and family picked me up at the airport, and from July 12 to July 16 they treated me to an experience I will never forget!

Gigi and her family were all so generous and caring. We went to a Swiss chalet high in the mountains for a fondue dinner and wine. Gigi's brother, Pierre, and his wife joined us. Gigi's aunt drove me up the winding road to the chalet in a sports car—what a great driver! On another day, Pierre took me to his private club up in the Alps. We even spent a day at the family's summer home in Lake Geneva. I am so happy for them, and they in turn are always wishing me happiness!

Later, in the mid-'80s, Gigi and René also visited with me and my mother at our home in Daly City. They were so kind to my Mama, and my mother understood why our *friendship* was so strong. This would be a better world if we could have more international friendships like these!

Gigi, Mama, and me when Gigi and
her husband visited us in Daly City.

After leaving Gigi and her family to continue my European vacation of July 1970, I took a bus to Nice on the French Riviera. Our Europabus drove via Annecy, Grenoble, Grasse, and Cannes. In Nice I stayed at the Negresco Hotel—a landmark hotel right on the Promenade, great for people watching. I had a table seat on the front entrance patio, and enjoyed watching the parade while sipping a glass of wine.

Around this time was when Al Bava and I used to lunch at the French cafe Le Petit on Grand Avenue in Oakland. Its charming owner, on hearing that I would be going to Nice on the French Riviera, had recommended that I rent a car and go to lunch at her friends' restaurant, L'Auberge de Gattieres. She had written the name and address on the back of her business card, along with a personal note written in French.

When I got to Nice, I rented a car and drove on the *very fast* roads to the village where this restaurant was located. But upon entering the restaurant, I saw they had a full house! The owner approached me and said that she was sorry that there weren't any tables available—in fact, they had no turnover at all, because guests just relaxed and ate and drank leisurely. I told her I was so disappointed, and that my friend from Oakland had told me that I must have lunch at her wonderful establishment. Then I showed her the famous business card.

Well, as soon as she read the personal note, she escorted me into the restaurant and welcomed me with open arms! What she did next was great: she "created" a table for me using a small table that had been holding a flower vase! Everybody around me greeted me with "welcome" in their native languages—Italian, Belgian, Parisian, and dialects from other French locales.

By the time I left the restaurant, I had a marvelous French menu signed by all the guests. One even composed a song with musical notes. And one of the guests had an electronics company in Paris and a villa in the town of Villefranche-Sur-Mer—where I was headed to spend the night!

Well, how did I get my menu signed by these wonderful international friends? I will never forget not only the marvelous French meal, but also the lively conversation—I used my Italian and English. The electronics company owner ordered French champagne for all of us. After those bottles were finished, I ordered "champagne for everyone"—including the wonderful owner and even the French waitress, who sat on top of my table!

Soon, the other guests ordered more champagne! We closed the place! The Parisian couple invited me to stay with them at their villa and leave the next morning after breakfast. They were so gracious and kind.

The villa overlooked the Riviera and had a marvelous garden. What a great way to live! I thanked God for the chance to have such a wonderful experience.

You see, I was never alone!

Next on the itinerary, I took a Europabus via the Italian Riviera to Genoa, Italy. En route, I was fortunate to meet an Italian couple who at the time lived in Argentina. (The husband was retired from a high-ranking financial position in Argentina.) They took me on a personal tour of Genoa and pointed out the historical significance of this powerful city. We also ended up exchanging Christmas cards for years. More international flavor to my list!

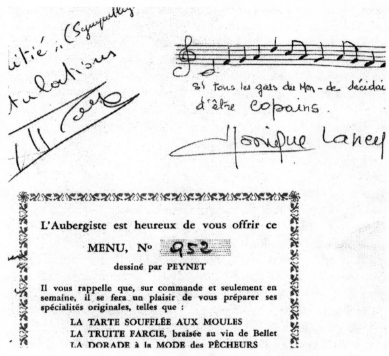

A corner of my souvenir menu from L'Auberge de Gattieres, signed by all the guests.

After Genoa, our tour group proceeded to Florence via Viareggio and Pisa. I had purchased a Bolex ZOOM movie camera while I was in Geneva with Gigi and René, and I had been using it during my month-long vacation. It was fun to be able to zoom in and out. Now I was able to climb to the top of the Tower of Pisa and create some great movies.

In Florence, during an outing on my own, I met a beautiful Italian girl at a sidewalk café. After dinner in the piazza, I walked her down the city's narrow streets to her home, where she lived with her parents. However, when I attempted to find my way back to the piazza, I got lost!

Nobody was around as I walked in and out of alleys. It was getting late and I was getting concerned. All of a sudden a man on a bicycle appeared, and stopped and walked me out of the "maze." I thanked him! He replied: "We are all brothers under God." I surely felt God was with me!

Next we proceeded to Venice via Ravenna. I had been there before while I was stationed in Austria, but I loved Venice once again. It is so beautiful, with the orchestra playing music in St. Mark's Square. I went to the internationally famous Harry's Bar for dinner and drinks. I met people from all over the world there. Just listening to the din, you could hear the different languages.

Then to Rome by Italian *rapido* train—they really run on time! This time I took movies of Pope Paul VI. Before when I was in the service, I had seen Pope Pius XII.

My last stop was *glorious Paris*! My hotel was again a "value" hotel costing something like $12 a night, including a continental breakfast. However, there wasn't an elevator, so I climbed up the stairs with my luggage—no problem. The hotel was named the London Palace Hotel. It was located near the opera house and many great sidewalk cafes.

I remember one night in Paris it was raining, and I was out on the town enjoying a great chateaubriand dinner under the restaurant's awning—what a marvelous feeling. The rain made the experience even better!

The French people treated me royally. The hotel, as I mentioned earlier, included a continental breakfast. However, one morning I left early to catch a tour and I skipped breakfast. So when I returned in late afternoon, I noticed on a table in my room a beautiful peach (*juicy* and *sweet*) with a note: "We are sorry we missed you this morning, but thought you would enjoy this peach on your return." I will never forget that kindness! The French are great, no matter what stereotypes you may hear.

I made more international friends a couple of years later, when I took an exciting "Orient Escapade" tour for twenty-one days, from July to August 1972. The trip included air transportation, tours, hotels, and meals for a total cost of about $1,300! I also had letters written on my behalf to representatives in Japan and Hong Kong. For instance, an executive from a company that provided janitorial services for Kaiser's high-rise buildings wrote to an acquaintance of his in Tokyo, a Mr. Asaji, requesting that I be given a tour of one of their Tokyo buildings, along with any other courtesies Mr. Asaji could offer. These letters really opened doors, as you'll soon see!

The entire trip was incredible—so different from Europe. It was truly an education. On my first night in Tokyo, after a very long flight over the Pacific, I found a card by the phone in my hotel room, which said something like, "Call if you would like a massage to relax." So I called! A very petite Japanese masseuse arrived, and once I had ushered her in, she had me lie face down, then proceeded to walk upon my back! It felt wonderful—what a great massage, and a nice way to start my adventure.

While I was in Japan, I was treated *very well* by Mr. Asaji and the janitorial services company. I was able to see a lot of sights that were not included in the paid tour. For instance, I went to nightclubs and even a geisha house!

After Japan we went to Taipei, Taiwan, where I visited the great National Palace Museum. Our next stop, Bangkok, Thailand, was really different: floating market tours, floating house boats, temples, and Buddhists.

In Hong Kong, I went to a shop and purchased a Minolta camera and a jade ring. In Oakland before my trip, my Chinese travel agent had written in Chinese characters the name of the jewelry shop and a personal message to the shop owners, who were the parents of her friend. Now in Hong Kong, getting to the shop was a great adventure!

First, the hotel doorman told the taxicab driver where to go. Then the driver took me to a distant neighborhood, where he stopped the cab and let me out. Everything around me was written in Chinese—no English! I had to match the characters on the card to a sign at one of the shops. Luckily I matched the right one.

In Hong Kong with some of the locals.

At the shop, I bought a custom-made jade ring—I picked the stone and I designed the ring. The owners then brought me to a family Chinese nightclub—what a feast! And the next day my ring was ready!

But the real excitement of this whole tour happened on our way back to the States, on the airplane. We were supposed to fly direct from Hong Kong to Hawaii, for a few days of rest and relaxation after the tour. However, after taking off from Hong Kong, we heard two explosions! The pilot came on the loud-speaker and announced that we had lost not one but *two* jet engines. And the next thing the pilot said is that he would have to *crash land* the plane in Tokyo!

Everyone prepared for the worst, and the pilot emptied the fuel tanks to minimize the risk of fire. Then, at midnight, our plane descended on the Tokyo airport. Suddenly, *kaboom!* The plane wheels slammed down onto the runway with an impact so heavy you could feel it in your bones. The landing gear screeched down the runway—it was a *really rough* crash landing. Once the plane came to a stop, we all followed emergency procedures to exit the plane immediately. Thank God we were safe!

We stayed overnight in Tokyo, and I was asked to be in charge of the group, since we no longer had an official tour guide to lead us (our guide had stayed in Hong Kong since the tour had essentially ended there). The next day we left for Hawaii—same pilot, *same plane*. But the engines had been repaired, and the pilot came on the loudspeaker now to announce that drinks were on the house! Everybody started drinking, and soon we were all relaxed and having pillow fights—it was a *release* from the tension caused by the crash landing. In Honolulu they let us pass without having to go through customs. Let me tell you, I will never forget that whole experience. Thank you, God!

Two of my cherished "international friends," Ralph and Connie Weber, helped me get through a critically sad time in my life—the period following the loss of my Mama, who passed away on February 19, 1997. She would have been ninety-six years old on April 24. I was extremely close to my Mama, and I was with her to the end, holding her hand.

I had retired from Cushman & Wakefield at the end of 1992. My Mama was requiring more personal attention in her nineties, and I decided it was a very pre-cious time to spend with her. This was more important than making more money! I had a chance to have quality time with Mama. John Renard, President of Cushman & Wakefield, had offered me other opportunities and told me I could return at any time. He was my hero! I even received an invitation to the *very swank* 1997 Cushman & Wakefield Christmas party, though I was no longer an employee there, and I had a great time attending. Almost a year after the loss of my Mama, I was beginning to feel like doing things again.

As the summer of 1998 approached, my dear friends Ralph and Connie Weber, who live in Heidelberg, Germany, offered to take me on a personally escorted tour of Germany and the Alsace, France, region. Ralph and Connie wanted to help me recover from the loss I had experienced, and I was ready for a vacation. I decided to join a Tauck tour called "Classic Italy," from June 13 to June 26. Then from June 26 through July 7, I would be in the Webers' hands.

This nearly month-long vacation turned out to be marvelous! The Tauck tour included a diverse group of people from all over the United States. We explored Sorrento, Rome, Umbria, Tuscany, Florence, and Venice. We visited San Gimignano in the Tuscany region, and the Cinque Terre—five remote Mediterranean villages. I purchased paintings and gifts from an American artist in San Gimignano.

It was a thrill in Venice to go to Hotel Europa & Regina by a boat shuttle. And Sorrento was so romantic—you could see why so many go there for a honeymoon. For that matter, all of Italy is a "love experience"!

One night at Harry's Bar in Venice, I met and talked to "Fonzie" (Henry Winkler). He was so gracious!

Our tour group was cohesive, and we enjoyed being together. One couple in particular, Crispina and Ian McDonald, were wonderful to be with, talking, touring, and dining together. We still exchange Christmas cards each year. They live very full and exciting lives and share their yearly adventures in a newsletter. Such a caring and intelligent couple!

After the end of the Tauck tour, Ralph and Connie Weber treated me to a trip of a lifetime. Imagine, driving through Germany and the Alsace region in a Mercedes sedan! We stayed at bed-and-breakfasts and hotels that Ralph and Connie were personally acquainted with from their own vacations.

You may recall the name Ralph Weber—he was at Fort Ord at the same time I was, and was also chosen to serve as an interpreter in Europe. He was sent to Germany while I was sent to Austria.

During the trip, Ralph's wife, Connie, kept a handwritten "diary" of our journey in great detail. We went to churches, castles on the Rhine (traveling in our car on the Rhine Ferry), wineries, and so much more. And Connie did an excellent job of recording the marvelous experiences—what a wonderful gift to me. By reading her notes, I can look back and see how busy we were, and what we did and experienced on each day. For instance, I can see that I bought five cuckoo clocks in Bacharach as gifts on July 1. This travel journal, along with the many pictures I took, brings back wonderful memories!

When I returned home after this memorable trip with my friends—both old and new—I felt a new energy! I was ready to go out and experience more of the world.

Top: My friends, Ralph and Connie Weber, during our tour
of the Alsace region. Bottom: Connie and
Ralph with the Mercedes. What a wonderful trip!

Practice 9

It has been said that meeting new friends can be like dating. If you are interested in meeting new friends, consider the following. First, make a list of activities that you enjoy or are heavily involved in. Next, write down places associated with those activities. For instance:

Reading—Bookstores, Library

Photography—Museums, Photo Labs

Childcare—Playgrounds, Schools, Toy Stores

Consider visiting these places and approaching others who may have similar interests. A good way to start is by asking a nonthreatening question, such as "Can you recommend a good Italian cookbook?" to someone who is browsing the cookbook section. You may just spark a friendship!

CHAPTER 10
BROADEN YOUR HORIZONS

I have been very lucky to travel extensively. Travel can be so rejuvenating, as I found in the year following the death of my Mama. It can also teach us what can't be learned in any school: firsthand experience of other cultures and people. I always recall the handbook I received when I began my work with the Inspector General in Austria, and its emphasis on respecting local cultures, people, and traditions—this is so important. In fact, when traveling, I've found that adopting this attitude will get you far!

Travel When You're Young

I have always enjoyed getting out and about. Even in high school and college, I enjoyed exploring California, both north and south, whether with friends and family or by myself in my Mercury. It was such a pleasure to go on "Sunday drives" when people toured at a *leisurely pace*.

Can you believe that gasoline once sold for twenty-five cents a gallon? And this was full service—the attendant would check oil and tire pressure, and clean windshields. On top of this, the gas stations gave blue-chip stamps, which were redeemable for nice gifts. They would also give away drinking glasses.

I loved the California coast, and I would sometimes put two suitcases in my trunk and drive down the coast and back for two weeks. I felt so free! People were friendly, and the pace was slower. We enjoyed talking, laughing, eating, dancing—we felt so young!

One year, around 1960, I drove all the way down to Ensenada, Mexico. What an adventure, driving Highway 1 along the spectacularly beautiful California coast. I stopped in coastal towns and cities like Carmel, Monterey, Malibu, Santa Monica, Hollywood, Newport Beach, La Jolla, San Diego, Big Sur, and Nepenthe. In Ensenada, the people were warm and generous. I ate at the home of fishermen and went fishing with them. And we talked! I was really meeting people from all over. The freedom, the beauty—that marvelous sense of discovery was always there.

Top: My brother, Joe, and me on a family outing in the 1960s.
Bottom: Mama and Papa preparing the picnic.

In the other direction, Lake Tahoe and Reno were favorite destinations for me and my family. On the long drives up and back, we would stop off at the Nut Tree Restaurant near Vacaville to eat—it was a tradition. And my brother, Joe, remembers the wonderful Giant Orange juice stands on the way to Lake Tahoe and Reno from the San Francisco Bay Area. The juice stands themselves were actually *round* and *orange*, selling delicious ice-cold, fresh orange juice.

In September of 1962, at age seventy-three, my Papa passed away unexpectedly. He had needed a blood transfusion because of a bleeding ulcer, which should have been treatable—but unfortunately he contracted hepatitis from the transfusion, and never made it out of the hospital! For my Mama and the rest of my family, this was a very sad period. So it was some time after this sad event that I decided to treat my mother to a Lake Tahoe vacation.

At this time, I was working at Kaiser Center in Oakland. So before we went, I had my car serviced in Oakland and had the technicians put on new brakes. I didn't want to take any chances: Highway 50 going to and from Lake Tahoe is narrow and steep, and the drop down the mountainside is huge!

We had a wonderful time in Tahoe, and when we came back it was downhill all the way. I was driving, my mother was in the back seat, and next to me in the front was my brother-in-law, Pete (my sister had married Pete Crosetti, related to Frank Crosetti of the New York Yankees, in 1946). We were going downhill at a slow speed, when all of a sudden I felt the brakes giving out! But I was stunned: I couldn't believe this was happening with *new brakes*. Then the car started going *faster* and *faster* downhill—I soon realized I had no brakes whatsoever!

Pete must have seen my face. He asked if I had a problem, and I answered that I was going to have to find a spot to pull over. Then I told them, *Brace yourselves* for a *hard stop*—hopefully a *safe* stop! In my mind I was thinking, *God help us!*

All of a sudden a turnout in the side of the mountain appeared. I whipped over into it and put on the hand brake, and turned off the engine. We were safe, thank God!

Once we had all calmed down some, I was able to flag down someone going toward Tahoe who could alert a tow company and the police. Our prayers were answered, and the tow truck arrived and took us to a service station. The mechanic at the station examined the brakes and reported that the brake fluid had leaked out from my new brakes! Fortunately, he was able to make repairs and replace the brake fluid, and we went home safely. Again, God was with us!

Later I went to the service station that did the brake job, and they denied any fault. I never did any more business with them, of course. But I was so happy that we survived. *Lesson learned:* Be calm, be positive—don't think about the bad but emphasize the good—and *trust in the Lord!*

Top: My nephew Ronald Crosetti, Marianna, and her husband, Pete Crosetti, in the 1970s. Pete served in both Japan and Europe during World War II, and married my sister after returning to Bernal Heights, where he too had grown up. Bottom: Marianna and Ronald in front of Ron's amazing collection of sports memorabilia.

I was able to continue traveling throughout my career, both by using vacation time and by working travel into my business activities. Often after a business trip to an interesting city, I would try to do some touring and further travel, if I had the time. For instance, after the Portland, Oregon, BOMA International Convention, I took some vacation time to tour Seattle, Washington, in July 1962. This was the time of the World's Fair there, with the opening of the famous Space Needle. It was very exciting to go to the top of the Space Needle and enjoy lunch on the rotating "Eye of the Needle."

I want to share with you my checking-in experience at the hotel in Seattle. When I got to my room, I noticed drapes across a window area. While the luggage was being brought in, I opened the drapes to see my view—what a shocker! It was a *brick wall!* I changed rooms for a better vista. And after this I always made sure to check my room before the baggage handler left!

After Seattle I visited charming, beautiful Victoria, British Columbia, staying at the famous Empress Hotel. Then on to Vancouver—an outstanding city! My hotel was overlooking the harbor and was near the Old Town, famous for its restaurants and music nightclubs. (Old brick buildings had been converted into a successful entertainment and dining center.)

I had a close call after a great time in Old Town, dining and listening to wonderful music groups. It was early in the morning, after midnight, and I decided to walk to my hotel a few blocks away. There was no taxi available at that time, and besides, my hotel was not very far.

As I walked, I noticed nobody was around except two young men who were walking toward me—*straight on*. Their body language made it clear they didn't intend to let me continue! As soon as they came up to me, one of them said, "What are you going to do about it?" His partner got behind me. I knew I was in trouble, and I prayed to Jesus and Saint Michael (in fact, in my mind's eye I saw his sword!). As I sensed the danger, I squeezed the arm of the fellow in front of me *so hard* that I felt his bone. He was so surprised at my strength, and yelled in pain. Then the two of them ran away! God was with me, without a doubt. I returned safely to my hotel.

Later that same year, I traveled in the opposite direction: I made arrangements to take a tour of Mexico from December 26, 1962, through January 13, 1963. Howard Travel Service in Oakland was preparing my schedule when they called me at my office in Kaiser Center to inform me that the Mexican visa office had classified me as a "Persona non Gratis" (not welcomed). This was a shocker! I had to submit documents that showed I served in the Army in Austria and was classified for "Secret Clearance."

Well, it turns out that the Mexican authorities had me *mistaken* for a Mafia member! I'm not sure if this was just because I am Sicilian, or if there was more to it. I have my own theory: the famous mobster Lucky Luciano had a financial adviser named Rubino back in the 1950s, and you may recall that around that time I happened to stay at the Grand Hotel et des Palmes in Palermo, Sicily—a hotel used by Luciano as his headquarters!

At any rate, I was fortunate to have our American Embassy to vouch for me. I was eventually cleared and *welcomed* to Mexico. At one point there had been talk that I should go under a different name. I'm glad I declined this move and traveled under my real name. I had one of the best times of my life in Mexico—my first trip!

This was a personalized tour that involved sharing a private car with another couple. That other couple turned out to be Max Factor and his wife, of the famous cosmetics firm! We had a marvelous, interesting trip. Imagine: we would check in to our accommodations by driving our limousine to the front entrance!

Our itinerary first covered Mexico City, Cuernavaca, Taxco, Vista Hermosa, and Acapulco. Then we took a three-day trip to Oaxaca where I purchased the famous "black pottery" from a well-known woman artist. I treasure my "fish pottery."

From Oaxaca, we moved on in our private car to Queretaro, San Miguel Allende, Guanajuato, Morelia, Lake Patzcuaro, Janitzio Island, and San Jose de Purua. What an education: beautiful art surrounded by beauty and wonderful history. I enjoyed sharing all this with the Max Factors.

In July 1968, I returned to Acapulco, Mexico, for a terrific vacation. I stayed at the Acapulco Hilton and sent a postcard home that says it all: "Right on the beach of Mexico's Riverside. 435 air-conditioned guest rooms and suites with private balconies overlooking Acapulco Bay and the lovely gardens." I wrote on the card that the swimming pool was circular, with a cabana in the middle.

At my hotel, I met people from all over the world. We would meet in the lobby and make plans for dinner and other activities. One day a lovely lady asked me to go sailfishing with her. Kay was from Chicago, and we had been sharing experiences in Acapulco. I accepted, naturally!

We left the hotel early in the morning, and Captain Ramos took us out to different locations, trying to find a good spot for catching fish. The boat was just for Kay and me. Well, the captain must have found the right spot: Kay and I each caught a sailfish at the *same time*! Really exciting! The captain had to maneuver the boat for both of us. It took over an hour, but we each caught our sailfish! They were huge, and Kay's was even longer than mine.

Back on shore, we had our fish weighed, and made arrangements for taxidermy. We also received certificates signed by Captain Ramos and a witness; these recorded the exact size of the fish. Mine was 8 feet long and 115 pounds. I believe Kay's was 9 feet and 120 pounds!

I really appreciated being asked by Kay to join her on this adventure; this has been a great lifetime memory. I used to display my fish in my office (it was quite an icebreaker), and I now have it in my den office in my home.

Showing off my eight-foot-long sailfish in
my office at Kaiser Center.

On another day during my trip to Acapulco, a few friends and I chartered a
sailboat, and it was marvelous. We sailed over to other beaches and had a grand
celebration! However, we went out so far that by the time we got back to our
hotel, the sailboat could not dock near our shore—the tide had gone out and the
water was too shallow. We realized we would have to jump off and swim to shore.

Well, I jumped into the water and started to swim, but what happened next
was incredible: I got caught in a riptide! Not once, but twice! I almost drowned.
Each time I thought I had touched the beach, the sand would just crumble under
me. But God was with me: I didn't panic and I kept my mouth shut (which is
normally difficult for me!). Eventually my friends rushed to help me get my feet
on to the beach.

Later, I bought cognac for everybody and said, "Thank you, God!" I had made
many friends on this trip—in fact, we corresponded for years, and I even visited
them. Also, Kay and her mother visited me some years later in Daly City—wonderful friends!

Throughout the 1970s, I took several trips overseas: to visit Gigi and her family in Europe in 1970, for example, and to tour the Orient in 1972. But in the
summer of 1976, I really went "over seas": I took a wonderful Caribbean cruise
on the Italian *MS Carla C.,* of the Costa Line.

I would love to repeat this experience! Between June 26, 1976, and July 3, 1976, we visited Willemstad, Curacao; La Guaira, Venezuela; Port of Spain, Trinidad; Fort de France, Martinique; St. Thomas, Virgin Islands; and San Juan, Puerto Rico. We took tours at each location, and in Venezuela we took a marvelous full-day tour of Caracas. It was exciting—almost too exciting: I nearly got left behind from the tour!

Here's what happened: When the official Caracas tour ended, a lovely female passenger and I hired a taxi to take us to other sites that weren't included in the regular tour. Well, we told the taxi driver that after a great time together, we were ready to go back to the cruise ship. However, we then got involved in a terrific traffic jam! The driver told us he would do his best, but he might not be able to make it on time. We would have to make arrangements on our own to join the ship at the next port!

Luckily, God was with us. Just as we arrived at the port, the ship was *raising* the gangplank! But our friends on board started screaming for the crew to put the gangplank down, which they did—after some convincing. Once we got back on board, I bought drinks for everybody. It had been nerve-wracking, but it was all worth it! Memories are made of this.

The meals served on this cruise were amazing, with themed menus like "A Night in Paris" and even a dinner showcasing American specialties, to celebrate the bicentennial. Each night we had interesting dishes like escargot, sautéed frog legs, roast duck, shark fin soup, and prosciutto with cantaloupe. Remember, this was a friendly Italian crew. We were treated royally! I remember one night they had lobster, and the waiter brought me *two* delicious lobsters. I ate the whole thing!

The staff was just great, and planned everything beautifully. I recommend this wonderful cruise line: Costa Cruises!

My Caribbean cruise ended in Puerto Rico on Saturday, July 3, 1976—one day before the grand bicentennial celebrations going on all over the United States. The very next day, I was lucky enough to spend July 4, 1976, having the famous Sunday brunch at Brennan's Restaurant in New Orleans. The restaurant had a special menu "In commemoration of our nation's 200th birthday," and it was signed by the owners—a nice keepsake of this memorable day.

The place was packed, naturally, and I was standing in line waiting my turn. The host asked for names to add to the waiting list. But when he heard me say "Rubino," he asked, "You are Sicilian?"

I said yes!

He replied, "So am I. Follow me!"

He then proceeded to give me royal treatment, with a marvelous table overlooking the garden. He also recommended other restaurants and insisted I go to this Sicilian bakery early in the morning for coffee and fresh cannoli. I did go, and it was well worth it!

While in New Orleans, I also went to the Café du Monde: "the original coffee stand." They serve the famous Sicilian doughnuts like my Mama used to make. We called them *spingi*, and in New Orleans they refer to them as *beignets*.

One of the guests I met on the Caribbean cruise had recommended that I go to Antoine's Restaurant—very famous and wonderful. He gave me his business card and wrote a message for the host. He told me to go directly to the head of the line and present my card to the host. I did this, and I was immediately escorted on a personal tour of the restaurant and got a great table! Once I sat down, I ordered the Oysters Rockefeller and received my number. (The restaurant has been assigning this dish a number since they started making it, so you know you're the nth customer to order it.) I kept the number!

New Orleans was a grand experience: the food, the jazz, the history, and people from all over the world. I found warm, friendly people everywhere! I just pray that the city can rebuild after Hurricane Katrina, and again be a wonderful place to visit or live.

Travel When You're Experienced!

Some time after I retired and my mother passed away, I decided to start traveling again much like I had in my younger days. It had really been several years since I took a long trip! As you recall, one of the first trips I took during this period was with my friends, the Webers, in Europe. But I also took three tours within the United States that same year. I was keeping busy!

The first tour I embarked on in 1998 was a Tauck tour called "Florida Resorts & Walt Disney World," featuring some of the finest coastal resorts in all of Florida: the posh Boca Raton Hotel, Hawks Cay Resort, Marco Island Resort, and the spectacular Walt Disney World Swan.

We began the tour by visiting the famous Thomas Edison winter home in Ft. Meyers and Edison's beautiful botanical garden. We toured the Everglades, and I took pictures of alligators. Then we reached the southernmost point of the continental United States: Key West, Florida. In Key West, we visited the Harry Truman White House. I bought a picture postcard there of Lauren Bacall sitting on a piano with Harry Truman, in 1945. Great picture!

Key West was colorful and a fun place to visit—I took lots of pictures. One afternoon, we were having an early dinner outside on the deck of the Rooftop Cafe, when all of a sudden a *strong* wind blew the furniture all over the deck and actually *scooped my soup up* out of the bowl!

Our next stop was Boca Raton, where we enjoyed seeing all the luxurious boats. We proceeded from there to the Kennedy Space Center by bus, and the driver announced that he would be driving faster than usual, because he had just learned that a space shuttle was scheduled to land soon! We did make it in time to see the landing, and I got to take a couple of pictures—the shuttle looks like a small speck on the photos. I do remember the two *loud* sonic booms as it entered the atmosphere.

Our last stop on the tour was Disney World. What great fun! I was able to board a waterway shuttle from the hotel right to the park. I had dinner in the park at the Hollywood Brown Derby, a re-creation of the real one in Los Angeles. (Previously when I was in Los Angeles, I had had dinner at the "Original" with my brother, Joe.)

This tour ended in May 1998, after which I left for Europe to tour Italy and then have a wonderful time with the Webers. Then in August 1998, I took a very relaxing and picturesque tour of Cape Cod and the Islands. My sister Marianna encouraged me to take this trip—I'm glad she did! It truly was marvelous. We visited Newport, Martha's Vineyard, Nantucket, and Chatham, and went whale watching. The official itinerary said it all:

> New England is where America began! Her seafaring past remains beautifully preserved in the grey-weathered shingles of Cape Cod homes, the dunes dotted with lighthouses, the quaint harbors, the rose-lined country roads, and quiet Atlantic beaches. Cruise out to the legendary offshore islands—steeped in lore from whaling days and relatively unchanged since.

It was a treat to visit the Breakers, "the most palatial of all the estates in Newport, once the seaside summer 'cottage' of Cornelius Vanderbilt."

We also went to Plymouth, where the pilgrims first stepped ashore in 1620, and saw the famous Plymouth Rock. I encourage everyone to visit this region for the history and for relaxation.

In the fall of 1998, I took a fabulous Tauck tour called "The Ozarks & Branson," of Memphis, Little Rock, Hot Springs National Park, Lake of the Ozarks, and St. Louis.

I began by staying at the beautiful and famous Peabody Hotel in Memphis, where I witnessed the daily parade of ducks to and from the lobby's marble fountain. People from all over the *world* gather for this event!

Also in Memphis, I was captivated by a visit to Graceland, the home of Elvis Presley. I went to the marvelous museum, too, to see his cars and show outfits.

My only regret about my stay in Memphis was that I didn't think to look up Marguerite Piazza, who lives there with her family!

From Memphis, we went on to Little Rock, Arkansas, and to the capitol. It was great to see the portrait of a young Governor Bill Clinton. From there we continued to the resort town of Hot Springs, where we enjoyed a soothing whirlpool bath and massage.

Onward to Branson, Missouri—one of the country's most popular entertainment destinations. We saw Tony Orlando perform. I would love to revisit Branson and take in a week's schedule of shows. Our accommodations were at The Chateau on the Lake—magnificent!

Our final stop was St. Louis, where we stayed at the Hyatt Regency at the city's Union Station. (The train station was converted to a hotel and bustling shopping mall.) In St. Louis, we visited the Gateway Arch and rode a tram to the top of the arch for a spectacular view from 630 feet above the banks of the Mississippi River. You sit down in the tram and get out at the top—what an amazing structure!

In May 1999 I continued my travels by joining another Tauck tour with my great friends Frank and Val Terranova. The destination was New Mexico, which Tauck terms the "Land of Enchantment." It is! The region truly has a calming influence, and it is no wonder that so many artists are located there.

We visited Albuquerque, Los Alamos, Taos, and Santa Fe, and the itinerary summarizes the experience beautifully:

> New Mexico is known as the mecca for Southwestern art and architecture, images of turquoise and taupe blending landscapes with design. American Indian, Spanish, and European Anglo traditions are woven together forming the state's cultural heritage. Experience one of the world's great steam train journeys, explore ancient Anasazi cliff dwellings, and take a class in cooking or painting in Santa Fe. This is Tauck's New Mexico, the "Land of Enchantment."

I took the painting class in the studio of a local artist, of course.

In Taos, we visited the Kit Carson Home and Museum, where the great frontiersman lived for twenty-five years.

In Santa Fe, we stayed at the colorful Hotel Loretto and visited the Georgia O'Keefe Museum, "dedicated to her drawings, paintings, pastels, sculptures and watercolors inspired by the extraordinary New Mexican landscape." The sculpture gardens and studios in Santa Fe are something to behold. Santa Fe is so rich in art! I came away wanting to revisit.

The Loretto Chapel in New Mexico is home to the famous spiral stairway and rose window in the choir loft. The stairway is famous because of the mystery surrounding the man who built it and also the physics of its construction. The story goes that the Sisters of the Chapel made novenas to St. Joseph, the patron saint of carpenters, to solve their problem of finding a way to access the choir loft (carpenters had examined the space and determined that there was no room for a staircase, and told the Sisters they would have to resort to a ladder). But on the ninth day of prayer, a man with a donkey and a toolbox appeared and said he was looking for work. He completed the staircase—and then disappeared without thanks or even pay. The stairway construction was innovative for the time, and certain things about it still perplex experts today. It definitely has a *spiritual* history and feel to it!

During this tour of New Mexico, I celebrated my sixty-ninth birthday, on June 4, and the group signed a beautiful card for me. They were all so thoughtful!

I took another fabulous trip with Tauck Tours from July 27, 1999, through August 10, 1999: "Treasures of the Aegean, Northbound." We started in Athens, Greece, and toured Greece by bus prior to boarding the Windstar cruise ship to visit the Greek islands and Turkey.

This region was stunning. I was overwhelmed by the *sheer emotion* and *beauty*! Walking through and seeing ancient civilizations is such an emotional experience. And the beauty was something to behold and to remember for a lifetime! I tried to capture some of this marvelous beauty and history with my photography. You have to experience it yourself!

The boat trip on the Bosphorus was relaxing, and the historic waterway is a sight to behold—what beautiful architecture.

There was more to the trip than ancient civilizations, though: In Greece I noticed that everybody was using their cell phones!

Istanbul was friendly and captivating. I went to a carpet bazaar and purchased a silk rug, which today I have hanging in a frame in my living room. It is all silk and absolutely stunning. The workmanship and design are incredible—what a treasure! And what a souvenir of this incredible trip.

When I left Istanbul, I had little idea I would be back in the Mediterranean region again just a few months later—for a very memorable return trip to Sicily. I had not been there or seen my relatives there since 1953!

I have my friend Frank Terranova to thank for this marvelous return trip. Frank and I have been friends since we met in the Army at Fort Ord, Monterey, in 1952. I can always count on Frank for help! (Frank did not go to Europe in the fifties, but served in the United States—Texas and New Mexico.)

Frank had gone on a tour of Sicily with his wife, Val, in 1998 and enjoyed it tremendously. So the following year, he gave me a brochure describing the trip to Sicily being sponsored by the National Italian American Federation (NIAF) in 2000. I signed up—and then Frank wanted to return, so we decided to go together! For that matter, Frank asked if we could make a side trip to Rome, so we made arrangements to do so after Sicily.

The trip to Sicily was marvelous—and eye-opening. Remember, the last time I was there was in 1953. Imagine my surprise! In 1953 there were mules and carts. Now, in March of 2000, there were *superhighways* and *cars*!

Sicily is really a fascinating place for anyone to visit. Its natural landscape is breathtaking, peppered with citrus and olive groves, vineyards, palms, and other flora taking root in its fertile lands. Invaded time and time again by an endless procession of settlers and conquerors, the island and its resilient people are the result of a truly tortuous history. Sicily has been fought over and occupied by Phoenicians, Greeks, Romans, Arabs, Berbers, Spanish Muslims, Normans, not to mention Barbarians and Vandals. The legacy of this cavalcade of civilizations today is a diverse culture, as well as beautiful and varied arts and architecture.

The NIAF tour of Sicily allowed us to visit Palermo, Monreale, Caltanisetta, Taormina, Agrigento, and Siracusa. Then on the "free day," I hired a driver to take Frank and me to Trabia. I was hoping to find my family at the old addresses of 1953. I had with me some photos of both families (Greco and Rubino) that I had taken in 1953.

When we arrived in Trabia, we stopped on the main road of the town. It was filled with cars and well-dressed people and beautiful apartments—no mules or carts! Luckily, I spoke Sicilian and I was understood. The driver also helped to ask around where the Rubino and Greco families lived.

Eventually, one young man said he would take us to the apartment of the Rubino family, which turned out to be right on the *main street*. In 1953 there was no electricity or running water. This time I rang a *doorbell!* A pretty young lady appeared from the window of the upper flat, and I told her I was Mariano from San Francisco. The door opened, and here was my Aunt Rosa, who I had stayed with in 1953—though in a very different house. We embraced, and she started crying with joy (I cried, too!). Uncle Angelo had passed away at age eighty-five. Aunt Rosa was now eighty-six. The young lady upstairs was my cousin, a daughter of my relative Giacomo.

I shared my pictures of 1953 inside their house (complete with television, VCR, phone, etc.). Frank and I then went with my cousins to see the Santa Rosalia statue near the water, as I had done nearly fifty years before. I mentioned that we also wanted to look up my Mama's family, the Grecos, but the Rubino family did not know where the Greco family lived! So after saying good-bye to the Rubinos (and taking pictures), Frank and I proceeded with our driver to the 1953 address to try to locate Aunt Angela on my Mama's side. However, when we got to the area, we discovered that the street name was no longer being used!

(Later we learned that the street had been renamed for a priest, a Father Tonda, who is being considered for sainthood.)

I had an idea of where to search for the Greco family next. I told the driver to go to the "Enchanted Train Station" where I had met Aunt Angela in 1953. When he pulled up to the station, I went in and began asking about my Uncle Ignazio, who was married to my Aunt Angela. The Station Manager asked why I was looking for him. I replied, "He is my uncle, and I'm from America."

His mouth dropped open with surprise, and he said, "He is my uncle also!" He then proceeded to take us to the home. My uncle Ignazio (my Mama's brother) and my aunt Angela were still living in the same place, but the house and really the whole neighborhood had been remodeled, plus the street name had changed. I was so happy to have located them. Can you imagine how wonderful it was to have this Enchanted Train Station to guide us? Thank you, God!

The Enchanted Train Station at Trabia, Sicily, in 2000.

Top: Reunited with members of my Papa's family—
Aunt Rosa is next to me in the middle.
Bottom: I was so glad to have located my
Mama's family! The Station Manager
(who turned out to be my cousin) is on the far left,
and Aunt Angela and Uncle Ignazio are on
either side of me in the middle.

After that glorious day in Trabia, Frank and I were ready to go to Rome. Our hotel in Rome was centrally located near the Spanish Steps. We really got a chance to meet wonderful people not only on tour, but when we got left behind by a tour and "Rick" of Rick's Bar helped us get in touch with the tour guide. We ate at his bar restaurant and took pictures.

"Rick" and his business partner at Rick's Bar in Rome.

In Rome, we toured the important historical sites and went to restaurants where the locals ate—great food and great adventures!

Frank and I came away from this trip with marvelous memories and more: we had met two wonderful friends on the Sicily tour, Paul and Eva Comi. The four of us enjoyed talking and sharing our experiences at lunch and dinner during the tour. I began referring to Paul as "Chairman of the Board" (as Frank Sinatra was called)—he has had a fascinating life! Paul has acted in numerous films and TV shows, including original *Twilight Zone* episodes and an episode of *Star Trek* (the original series), and is very acquainted with the Hollywood scene. He is also involved with the Academy Awards organization.

Paul and Eva come to San Francisco each year for the gourmet foods show at Moscone Center, and Frank, Valerie, and I try to get together with them for dinner. One time Paul sent us a photo of himself in *Star Trek*, autographed. I had mine framed and then arranged to have it hung on the wall at our table at the Cliff House in San Francisco. (The walls at the restaurant have for years had autographed pictures of famous movie stars.) There it was when we arrived for dinner. Paul and Eva were delighted!

Frank Terranova, Paul Comi, and me during our memorable tour of Sicily.

Next on my travel odyssey, following Sicily and Rome, was a destination closer to home: I boarded a cruise ship for Alaska. We set off from Vancouver, Canada, on August 7, 2000, aboard the amazing *Sun Princess* of Princess Cruises. What an experience! The ship is a *hotel* on water. I had wanted to see what it would be like to be on a ship as huge as the *Sun Princess*. There are elevators, entertainment, restaurants, and people (lots of people)—a city in itself.

At dinner each night I enjoyed the company of an Italian couple from Milano: Franco and Mariuccia Fazio. They relied on me to act as interpreter for the other couple at our table who did not speak Italian. It was my pleasure to be an ambassador of goodwill! The Fazios invited me to visit them in Milano, where they own hotels. I just may take them up on it. Stay tuned!

Alaska itself was breathtaking, too: glaciers, eagles, beautiful lakes, and much more. "Sheer beauty and majesty" best describes the landscape—what a beautiful state.

Just a month after my Alaska trip, I joined a marvelous Tauck tour called "Canada's Capitals & Niagara Falls," from September 24 through October 3, 2000. We started in Montreal, where we visited the beautiful Notre Dame Cathedral. Then I had a new experience: at the Hilton Montreal Bonaventure, a movie was being filmed in the lobby, and I got to be an extra! It was great to meet with the actors and crew. I even attended a cast party at the hotel.

From Montreal, we visited the Montmorency Falls and toured the famous Shrine of Saint Anne de Beaupre.

Our next stop was Quebec, where we stayed at the stately Chateau Frontenac. Quebec is delightful with its Old World charm. I could have stayed there another week.

Onward to Ottawa, Canada's capital—especially beautiful and impressive! While we were in the glass elevator of the Parliament Building, we could see a lot of activity in the lobby. Soon we learned why: Prime Minister Pierre Trudeau had just passed away. People were crying and bringing flowers to place by his picture in the lobby and near the Centennial Flame. It reminded me of when President John Kennedy died. Prime Minister Trudeau was definitely loved! I saved pages from the *Globe and Mail*, a Canadian newspaper, which published a wonderful tribute.

After this experience, we visited the great city of Toronto and had very comprehensive tours, including the downtown and residential areas. From there we proceeded to *glorious* Niagara Falls. What a thrill not only to see the falls, but to go on the *Maid of the Mist* and sail right next to them—I really got very wet! They claim "there's magic in the Mist."

When I returned home from Niagara in the fall of 2000, I planned to continue traveling—but after the tragic events of September 11, 2001, I decided it was time to stay home for a while. I had gone on two or three trips each year since 1998, and I had really seen quite a lot!

Soon I also began to focus my attention on putting together this book. But there's another lesson I've learned about travel: it's addictive. So now that my book is complete, I plan to keep exploring the world around me, and making friends as I go.

My next stop? Stay tuned!

Practice 10

Write down the names of some places you'd like to visit—whether they're close to home or far away.

Visualize yourself visiting each one. Do you see yourself traveling alone, with a friend, or with a tour group? If you can (remember, be optimistic!), set a date to travel to one of these places, and start saving money and planning for it. And keep visualizing yourself achieving your goal!

About the Author

John Rubino was an executive with the Henry J. Kaiser organization for twenty-eight years and Vice President and Director of Marketing and Promotion for Cushman & Wakefield of California for nine. A tireless volunteer and positive force for civic improvement, he has also participated in numerous charities, organizations, and events in the Oakland, California, community. He lives in Daly City, California.

Heather Hutson Moro is a freelance editor and writer and a member of the Bay Area Editors Forum. She lives in Napa, California, with her husband and daughter.

RESOURCES

I would like to recommend the following resources, as they have been instrumental in my life. Materials like these can help you remain focused on what's important, cope with challenges, and develop and maintain a positive outlook—which I have found to be a wonderful asset. Happy reading!

Books

Acres of Diamonds, by R. H. Conwell (Paperback edition publisher: Jove, 1989)
A classic. In print as a book or an audiobook; check bookstores and libraries. Also available free as an e-book or to listen to as a speech on various Web sites.

A Touch of Wonder: Staying in Love with Life, by Arthur Gordon (Publisher: Revell, 1996)
In print; available as a book.

Psycho-Cybernetics: A New Way to Get More Living Out of Life, by Maxwell Maltz, M.D. (Publisher: Pocket, August 1989)
In print; available as a book or an audiobook.

Truths Men Live By: A Philosophy of Religions and Life, by John A. O'Brien, Ph.D., LL.D., The University of Notre Dame (Publisher: Kessinger, May 2005)
In print; available as a book.

How to Make Positive Imaging Work for You
What Motivation Can Do for You
You Can Have God's Help with Daily Problems
Positive Thinking for a Time Like This
Treasury of Joy and Enthusiasm
All by Norman Vincent Peale. These particular books by Norman Vincent Peale are no longer in print, but can be found used. Other NVP books that have become classics, such as *The Power of Positive Thinking,* are still in print—I recommend these too!

The Dynamic Laws of Prosperity: Forces that Bring Riches to You, by Catherine Ponder (Revised edition publisher: DeVorss & Company, June 1985)
In print; available as a book or an audiobook.

The Bible!

Papers and Articles
Ordinary Olympians: The Secrets of Superior Performance, by Marilyn King, *In Context: A Quarterly of Humane Sustainable Culture,* Winter 1988, p. 14
Available from context.org

Young Millionaires' "Can Do" Attitude, by Gregg Levoy, San Francisco Chronicle, October 19, 1987
May be available on microfiche at Bay Area libraries.

Seven Steps to Career Success: How to Become One of the Top People in Your Field, by Brian Tracy, President and Founder of the Institute of Executive Development
Available from briantracy.com

Philosophy of a Happy and Successful Life, by Henry J. Kaiser
From the introduction written by Dr. Norman Vincent Peale:

> Industrialist Henry J. Kaiser delivered the layman's Sunday sermon on October 16, 1949, at the Marble Collegiate Church in New York City. Each year a famous Christian layman is invited to fill this historic pulpit. The overflow congregation filled three auditoriums to hear his inspiring message.... So tremendous were the requests for copies, that his sermon is here published for wide distribution.

Originally distributed by Peale's organization. No longer distributed today, but if you can find a copy in a library or bookstore, it is well worth reading! Or consider contacting a company associated with Peale's organization, such as dailyguideposts.com, to inquire about obtaining a copy.

Inspirational Notes
The following are classics available for reading on the Internet.

The Optimist Creed, by Christian D. Larson, 1912

Fireplace Motto, by Henry Ford

Do You Remember Who Gave You Your First Break? (Author unknown)

978-0-595-68210-2
0-595-68210-3

Printed in the United States
81338LV00004B/190-198